SOMEBODY'S DAUGHTER

SOMEBODY'S DAUG

SOMEBODY'S DAUGHTER

A MEMOIR

ASHLEY C. FORD

THORNDIKE PRESS
A part of Gale, a Cengage Company

LIBRARY OF CONGRESS CIP DATA ON FILE.
CATALOGUING IN PUBLICATION FOR THIS BOOK
IS AVAILABLE FROM THE LIBRARY OF CONGRESS.

ISBN-13: 978-1-4328-9056-8 (hardcover alk. paper).

Published in 2021 by arrangement with Flatiron Books

Printed in Mexico
Print Number: 01   Print Year: 2022

For my family,
and my friends who feel like family

Although the wind
blows terribly here,
the moonlight also leaks
between the roof planks
of this ruined house.
— IZUMI SHIKIBU

Ashley,

I must admit that I was surprised to hear from you. I had just come in from my institutional job, when one of the correctional officers brought me my mail. I thought that it was a book or newspaper that I had ordered, because I hardly ever, if ever, receive any mail from anyone on the streets.

Ashley, don't take this the wrong way, but come next year, I will have been incarcerated for twenty years, which means the letter that you wrote to me is the first letter that you have written me in almost twenty years. I was at a loss for words as I slowly read your letter over and over again.

You are right when you say that you are a woman now, and not a little girl. So, I won't talk to you like you are a little girl. Instead I will talk to you like you are a woman. However, don't misunderstand me, you will always be my little girl, not to mention, my favorite girl.

Why God in heaven gave you to me, only he knows. I do not deserve to have you as my daughter, but God gave you to me for a reason, and I am so grateful to be your father. Please! Please! Forgive me for all the pain I caused you in your life.

I am going to survive prison. I am going to create a beautiful life for myself. I'm going to show you and your brother R.C. how much I love you with every breath I take. Ashley, your father is coming home. I cannot promise you when that will be, but I can give you my word that I am coming.

Love always,
Dad

1

"Just remember, you can always come home."

There it was. I expected and hated when my mother said those words. Two years before this call, I'd moved to Brooklyn from Indiana. Now I lived in Flatbush with my boyfriend, Kelly. Back home in the Midwest, our friends were building four-bedroom houses on one-acre lots with mortgages comparable to the monthly rent of our one-bedroom. After living in the city for a year or two, I marveled at home features I would have called standard before I left. Features like dishwashers, in-unit laundry, and backyards. The apartment we lived in now had one of those, the dishwasher. When it ran, the second phase of the wash cycle shook the floor and walls with a deep rumble. I felt it in my feet while I paced the floor.

I had gotten up from dinner to take the

call from my mother. She still lived in Fort Wayne, my hometown. We hadn't lived in the same city, or the same house, since I left for college eleven years earlier. She called every few weeks — I answered every other call — and we usually had a good time talking for ten to fifteen minutes. I'd taught myself to keep our phone conversations light, or as I liked to think of it, complication-free, without lying. I didn't want to lie to her. I wanted to be able to talk to my mother the way I could with most other people, as myself. But she wasn't just anybody. She was my mother, so that was impossible. There were limits. We only dove into subjects that wouldn't end in arguments, which was mostly whatever would make us both laugh.

When she said that thing to me, that I could always come home, part of me wanted to reply, "Mama, I love you, but I'll work myself past the white meat, down to the bone, and fistfight every stranger I run across on the street before we live under the same roof again." That was the hyperbolic expression of a feeling I did not allow myself to verbalize, for fear of ruining our smooth interaction. And it would have. There was no way to make it sound like a joke because in some way, I wasn't joking. I got angry with myself for even thinking the thought because I knew it would hurt her to know it had ever been in my mind. I got mad at myself too, for not saying it out loud anyway. For not caring if it hurt her, if it meant telling the truth.

Before she called, Kelly and I were eating. We were lovers who lived together, trying to find out if we had whatever turned two people in love into the kind of family either of us wanted. We decorated and burrowed into our apartment, The Nest, as he began to call our tight, warm space. We hung cheap framed prints on the walls, topped bookshelves with action figures and small stuffed animals. We created a barricade between our softest selves and the sharp elbows of the city surrounding us. It wasn't that we couldn't take a hit, we just weren't used to the pace, but we still believed we could figure it out. Either way, we were finally home, in *our* home together, and I felt protected by our walls and the love shared there between them.

In our small kitchen, I wanted to cook for everyone and anyone, which mostly ended up being Kelly. It was a developing skill, but to my surprise, I was not a disaster. It was one of the ways I was learning to soothe myself, suggested by a therapist who told me, "Take the time to feed yourself food that feels good and tastes good. Who better to do that for than you?" It felt like exactly the kind of thing you pay someone to say to you. I still did it. Losing myself in the construction of a meal was the closest thing I had to a hobby.

The night my mother called, I made pasta. I tried to prepare the food to be served hot and ready minutes after Kel walked through the door. He would have eaten my pasta at any temperature I offered it to him, but I wanted to get it right. When he closed the bookstore where he worked, he didn't get home until nine forty-five p.m. at the earliest, closer to ten if he had to count the drawer more than twice. My timing didn't always work out, but this evening I pulled it off. Our plates were piled with thick ropes of linguine in a homemade garlic tomato sauce, oozing from the ends of our forks.

When my phone buzzed on the counter, I'd squinted at the screen before answering. I'd been trying to spend less time holding or even looking at my phone. Kelly could walk away from his phone for half a day before remembering it existed. Engaging with various social media platforms didn't appeal to him the same way. He often asked me to put mine away to be present with him, especially during meals. He wasn't wrong to ask, and I did not resent the request unless it embarrassed me. I knew I spent too much time on my phone, but sometimes I wished he could ignore that as well as I could. Still, I loved and wanted to be present with him. The only reason I gave a second thought to answering the phone during our meal was that my mother had worked the same job for more than two decades, and these days, was almost always asleep by nine, if not before. Seeing her name flash across my phone's screen worried me, so I picked up.

"Hello, Mother," I said in a faux posh voice. It was meant to keep things as jovial as the moment could stand. Usually, she would respond with her own equally posh voice, "Hello, Daughter," then we'd both giggle and tell each other something silly, or gossip, or ask the question we'd called to ask. This time my mother said, "Hi, baby," and I knew this wasn't a quick gossiping call. I walked into the bedroom to be on my own.

I shut the door behind me, and sat on the bed. My chest was tight with anticipation for whatever she said next. I started to count my breaths the way my first therapist had taught me, but couldn't remember how long

I was supposed to hold the breath, or for how long I was supposed to let it out. I never thought enough about breathing until I needed to, and by then, it was too late. I've heard people describe panic as something that rises up inside them. For me, panic radiates in the threads of my muscles, bangs in the back of my skull, twists my stomach, and sets my skin on fire. It doesn't rise or fall. It spreads.

Was it one of my siblings? My worst fear was that my mother called to tell me something happened to either one of my two brothers, or my sister. Since high school, maybe even a little before then, I'd experienced recurring nightmares about one of them dying. Never dreamt of anything too gory, thank God. I never had to watch them die, not even in the worst iterations of my dreams. I always arrived in the aftermath, left to deal with the reality of losing them before waking and getting the chance to prove to myself my little loves were still here. My mother knew about my nightmares, and had sent me back to bed many times after I burst into her room to listen to my youngest brother's heartbeat, or watch my sister's back fall and rise with the deep and heavy, but living breath of sleep. The dreams intensified when I left for college, and again when I eventually left Indiana altogether.

Her voice pulled me back to our halting conversation. She reassured me from the other end of the phone line. "Nobody's hurt. Everybody's okay." The top half of my body collapsed with relief and I fell back onto the bed. I closed my eyes, and when that didn't shut out enough light, laid my forearm against my closed lids until the view behind them faded into purple and black like the climax of a bruise.

"So what is it, Mom?" I waited for her to speak, and cursed what felt like dramatic pauses under my breath. We'd never found an easy way to talk about hard things, so we struggled to say anything at all in hard times. If she was calling about money, I wished she would just ask for what she needed, so I could be honest about whether or not I could help, and we could be done. My mother huffed. She sensed my impatience. That I was an adult who was allowed to be frustrated with her annoyed her whether she verbalized it or not. For all the ways we chose to remain silent, communicating our displeasure never actually required words. She spoke.

"Your dad is getting out of prison."

My breath caught between my mouth and

lungs, unsure in which direction it was most needed. My heart hit the gas, rushing blood to parts of my body calling out for it, and my hands trembled. *What were those breathing counts again? Six in, six out? Six in, seven out?* Was I going to cry? I touched my face with a shaking hand to be sure I hadn't already started. Nothing. My mother didn't speak, and it no longer felt like a performance. It felt right to have all that space for my words, my feelings, whether or not they decided to show up and tell me how to respond.

My heartbeat traveled to every end of me, pumping pumping pumping through my ears. I moved my mouth enough to ask the only question presenting itself with any clarity in my mind, "When?"

"In about two weeks. I just found out he's coming home." She paused, and once again, I was grateful to have room for my thoughts. "Are you okay?" I wasn't, but I didn't want to have to keep talking about how I wasn't okay. It was a relief to know my siblings were unharmed, and she hadn't done or said anything wrong. The ends of her questions lingered like she really did want to help, and I believed she did. The issue was that I'd been waiting to hear that my father was getting out of prison my entire life, and now that someone called me and said it was happening, all I could feel was how much I wanted to get off the phone.

I was tempted, as I always am, to take the bait when my mother offers me empathy. Tempted by my fantastical belief that one day I will lower my walls, and she will do the same. Then I end up blaming myself for not remembering to stick to the conversational paths offering the least resistance, furious at myself for veering too far into the unexplored or exiled. Or worse, I'd be drawn into her fantasy that we were already close. If my mother and I shared anything without having carefully considered it, it was this undying ember of a dream that we will someday, somehow find ourselves reaping the bounty of a blooming mother-daughter bond, the roots of which we both refuse to tend in the meantime.

I told her I was okay. She didn't press me, and I offered nothing else. I wondered if maybe she didn't want my answers anyway, and the single thought was convincing enough for me to keep my mouth closed. I thanked her for telling me about my Dad, told her I loved her, waited to hear it back, and hung up the phone.

Dazed, I walked back to the kitchen counter and sat down beside Kelly, wanting nothing more than to be close to him. I didn't want to be touched, even as I begged myself not to cry. I laid my phone back on the counter, facedown. He was still finishing his meal, but stopped eating and turned to me. My head spun with words, images, bits of conversations, music, and colors making up a swirl of debris zipping past my face, and returning seconds later, moving too quickly for me to reach out and hold onto anything long enough to make sense of the patterns they made, or whatever they tried to tell me. If I'd had the option, I would have called my grandmother to tell her the news myself, and hear her shout, "God is so good!" as if she'd just put in a prayer request for this very outcome. She had been reliably religious, and though I never would be again, her exclamations of joy brought me comfort when I needed it most. I needed it now.

I tried to count again, to breathe, or at least go numb enough to speak without crying. My emotions moved through me faster than I could name them. Feeling any of it felt like the beginning of losing control, and losing control felt like certain death in my body, if not my mind. If I didn't process the feeling, I wouldn't feel it, and if I didn't feel it, it couldn't kill me.

"What was that about?" he asked. I picked up my fork and took a bite of my food. It was cold now. It was still good, but not perfect. I chewed, swallowed, and spoke without looking up.

"My dad's getting out of prison in two weeks." I kept eating.

Kelly quit moving and stared at me, his eyes popped open, and his jaw lagged a bit, before he snapped it shut again.

"Well," he asked. "How does that make you feel?"

"I don't know," I said. I looked down at my phone, wondering if I should call my mother back and say more, or ask more. But what would I say? What questions did I have that she could answer? If I knew the right words, or the right questions, I didn't trust myself to say them the right way. If I called back, even if I needed to call back, we would fight. I felt certain that was true. Then, I stopped eating, and despite my own internal protests, began to cry.

"Kel," I sobbed. "I really don't know how I feel." I sat on the stool, gulping air, and swiping at my tears. My boyfriend watched me, sat patiently beside me, and when I lowered one of my hands into my lap, he covered it with his own.

I felt like I knew my father, and I knew he

felt like he knew me too. In reality, we'd spent the majority of both our lifetimes mentally constructing versions of one another we couldn't physically confirm or deny the existence of. We dreamed of one another — what we might be like — long before we met. My uncle Clarence, my father's closest brother, used to stare at me when we were in the same room. Sometimes I caught him. "You gotta excuse me," he'd smile. A smile that felt familiar and safe from the beginning. "You look just like my brother, but smaller and with pigtails." Then he'd hug me, and we'd laugh to keep the sadness away. I always wished he'd say more about the little brother he loved, the man who left me with his face, and little else. He rarely did. I didn't see Uncle Clarence that often. I kept wishing anyway.

The few times I visited my father, though pleasant, bowed under the weight of our expectations. We were happy to see one another, but we could not always say the thing we wanted to say most and risk spoiling the other's dream. We never discussed them, yet somehow agreed on these terms. An unspoken pact between an emotionally desperate father and daughter. Made up contracts for a shoestring bond.

"That's okay, baby," my father would say,

when I tried to apologize on the phone for not writing. "You write me when you want to. I'll be waiting patiently, and happily."

He kept writing. He wrote that I was his favorite girl, I was brilliant, and I was the best daughter anyone could ever hope for. For a long time, that was all I needed. Until, of course, I needed more.

2

My oldest memory is of my younger brother, R.C., eating a smashed overripe tomato. I remember the way he grabbed at the pulpy red flesh, and the way he could only hold it one way: as tightly as he possibly could. This is normal for small children who have not yet mastered their motor skills. There is no difference between holding and squeezing. They don't know any better. He didn't know any better, and neither did I. Of course, the guts of the fruit broke free into the spaces between his small fingers, and made a mess on the white tray top surrounding him. By the time he opened his hand to take a bite, there were only cold strings of bright skin and small white seeds.

My brother was too young to walk, but I wasn't. It was I who rooted around in the bottom of the refrigerator, found the food, and attempted to slice it for him with a butter knife. He'd been crying in his walker, the little wheels scooting back and forth across the floor as he flung himself from side to side. My mother slept so hard his wails didn't stir her. I didn't want her to wake up. I wanted her to sleep, and I wanted to help. My brother and I were fourteen months apart in age, so I must have been around three years old. I don't remember a time before him. I was supposed to have been a miracle baby for my mother. She'd had an ovary removed as a teenager, and her doctor told her the other one didn't work. It worked enough for me apparently. Then R.C. came along, and I was not a miracle anymore. I was a big sister, and to me, that was better. I loved him too much right from the beginning.

I saw my mother go to feed him each time he cried, so I thought food would make him happy. He was my best friend. I would take care of him. I rubbed his head and whispered, "Don't cry, baby. Don't cry."

When I was in college, one of my therapists at the on-campus counseling center told me I shouldn't remember any of this because I was too young. He told me most people don't have memories of themselves or their experiences at two and three years old. He asked me when I started speaking. I told him that I could speak in sentences before I could walk, a fact I'd been reminded of by my grandmother every chance she got.

"You couldn't walk straight for nothing. We called you Stagger Lee!" She'd say, laughter ripping through her entire body, infecting anyone else in the room, even me, often at my own expense. "But you'd point at something you wanted and say, 'I want that!' I thought, what kind of child is this?" She'd shake her head, recreating the same confused look she'd apparently worn all those years ago.

I told him my grandmother had a tendency to oversell my childhood intellect, so I couldn't be sure if it was accurate information. He wrote it down on his notepad, and I continued to tell him my stories, or what I remembered of them. My earliest memories are sunburnt Polaroids, frozen moments gone blurry at the edges and spotted all down the middle. Then, at four, the pictures become clearer and clearer, as do the voices within them. The loudest voice belongs to my brother, before he could properly pronounce my name, calling for me.

"Hashy? Where are you? Where is my Hashy?"

My brother loved me and made it so easy to believe I was good. I was a child, unspoiled in a certain way. I didn't doubt myself. I decided and I tried. Then I'd fail and try again. Or I would succeed and go on to try something new. I was not always as afraid of the world or as nervous about the other people living in it alongside me, or what they might do to me. When my life was new, I understood in my bones how little it mattered what anybody else was doing, or what they thought about what I was doing. I believed my bones then.

When I was four years old, I taught myself to lie awake until morning. I wanted the sunrise, and I only had to stay awake to have her. When children are small, our desires seem small, even if we want the sky. Anything we want seems to be only a matter of time and effort away. It's too early to imagine what's already holding you back.

I'd been enraptured with a storybook about the cycle of the sun. I remember looking on in awe as my teacher outstretched her right arm, extending it as far as she could, her fingers spread for the illusion of an extra inch. Her left arm moved out and away from her body, though not as far as its opposite, still close enough to read from the book she held. It was a simple and sad attempt to describe the sheer enormity of a life-supporting star to a pre-K classroom.

She said the word "sunshine," and we said it back. Her eyes roamed the cramped space for something to support her lesson, a point of reference that might get this thing to click. The taupe tile floor, and its matching tattered and stained square reading carpet, had nothing to add. Nor did the sky, nor rain falling from overfull clouds inching down the window behind her. Still, she tried to get us to understand, to sit down, to stop talking, to want to know more about what the universe might be up to while life so far had been teaching us to be wholly consumed with ourselves.

I wanted to know. I sat quietly, and waited for her to continue the story of the sun. My teacher turned the second to last page, revealing the final illustration. Those massive swirls of orange, gold, yellow, and a smattering of sweet pinks left little cracks all over my heart.

I gasped.

I repeated the word "sunrise," and the sound opened like a spring bloom on the tip of my tongue. There are few words worthy of the wonders they describe, but sunrise sounds like it feels. A *u* sunken to the bottom of one's throat, and an *i*, pointing upward and onward to a warm beyond.

I'm sure I'd seen a sunrise sometime

before then, and had maybe even heard the word before. The sky was already one of my favorite things. It told me what kind of day I might have. A sunny day usually meant being outside with family, especially R.C., my brother, best friend, and favorite playmate. Sometimes our mama even played with us.

Rainy days were charming too. My mother, brother, and I would sit on the couch together, small limbs draped over big ones, and watch movies. We had four or five kids' movies on VHS and my brother learned them all by heart. Every once in a while, he would get lost in a movie, sitting, staring, and speaking every line of dialogue as the actors spoke it on-screen. My mother, grown frustrated, would yell, "Shut up or I'll turn it off!" He would stop. But after sitting a while, staring a while, and forgetting why he shouldn't, he'd start to do it again.

When she got tired of kid movies, my mother would put on something meant for older audiences. My brother and I would watch those too. My obsession with sunrises and sunsets was only stoked by their repeated appearances in the introductions or theme songs of some of my favorite television shows like *The Golden Girls* or *China*

Beach. I'd never noticed the sky above our home look anything like the orange and gold dreamsicle clouds in my teacher's book, but I'd seen them on TV. I knew they happened somewhere.

After school that day, on the car ride back to our apartment, I decided I wanted the sunrise. I knew I couldn't have the sunrise or its colors for my own. Some things were too precious not to be shared. They just had to happen, and you just had to make sure you were there when they did, and then, you were part of something with everyone else who showed up at the right time.

The first night I reached for the sun, my mother was expecting company. Mom, R.C., and I usually shared one bed in the studio, but she tucked us kids in on the couch that night. This put a huge kink in my plans. There was a window right behind the bed but not the couch. I'd glimpsed the leftovers of the brilliant painted sky many mornings when I woke up for school, but it wasn't good enough. I'd convinced myself it would look different, more brilliant, if I stayed up to watch. I wanted the real thing, and I knew I could prove myself worthy to the sky. *I want a sunrise, and so it shall be* was a natural truth in my child mind, and I did not let go.

The view from the couch wouldn't do. I tried to stay up anyway, to practice for the night after — but my brother's warm legs, wrapped up in mine under our blanket, brought on the dense and resolve-melting fog of exhaustion. My mind resisted rest, but all that closeness eventually soothed me to sleep.

The next morning, I woke up to the sun already in the sky and the television playing. A commercial was running and I caught the words, "Smoking cigarettes will kill you." I rubbed the sleep out of my eyes and looked over at the pack of cigarettes sitting in my mother's black purse. She must not have known. I sat up to tell her, but she wasn't in the room. I heard noises coming from behind the closed bathroom door, letting me know she was handling private business, but I couldn't wait for her presence or permission to act. I grabbed the cigarettes from her black purse, opened the small cardboard box, and dumped each one into the trash can full of last night's dinner, which has been prepared exclusively from cans. When my mother came out of the bathroom, I told her what I'd seen about the cigarettes on TV.

"They could kill you!" My mother rolled her eyes at me, and at the mention of them, began looking for her cigarettes in earnest.

Only then did it occur to me she may not feel relieved I'd already thrown them out.

I watched the panic sweep over her, as my own followed. When we were bad, my mother hit us for it, and there was always the thought that I would die in the back of my mind. I didn't think my mother wanted to kill me on purpose. It was her eyes. My mother's rage drained the light from her eyes, and she became unrecognizable to me. There was Mama, the loving mother we knew before whatever sparked her ire, and then there was Mother who showed up in her place. Mother felt separate, somehow apart from our otherwise happy and harmonious existence. She rose from somewhere within Mama and did the latter's dirty work. Every once in a while, my brother and I were the dirty work needing done.

I sat quietly on the couch watching my mother, trying to be very still. I knew Mama would find her cigarettes in the black trash bag eventually, a few of them ripped in half to ensure their loss. When she did, I was going to get hit, and I was already afraid of the pain.

I couldn't, and I wouldn't, tell on myself. Self-preservation had already been imprinted upon me as a requirement. Honesty was not always the best policy. Grown-ups would tell you it was important to tell the truth, and when you did, everything would work out, but I knew this wasn't the case.

There must have been a time before, a time when I'd done something bad, realized it, and told on myself. The punishment I received for the forgotten transgression must have been severe, because the next time I was alone and I did something bad, it belonged only to me. I learned to carry the secrets of my badness silently and alone. There would be no more confessions from me. Whoever wanted to know how bad I could be would have to get close enough to find out, and nobody tried.

My mother didn't stop searching for her cigarettes. I hoped, for a moment, she might question if she'd actually been the one to throw them away. These things happened accidentally. That would have been lucky for me, but I did not feel like a lucky child. I saw too much and suspected even more than that. I waited for what I knew would come.

The day dragged on, heavy from the weight of my mounting fear. That night I fell asleep before the sun rose again, exhausted from the nervous energy coursing through my body. I woke in a vise. I was being squeezed on all sides, and the television was too loud. There were people screaming on whatever show was playing, and I couldn't understand why my mother didn't turn it off. The voice was too close, and the vise was too strong for me to linger in the space between sleep and awake.

"Ashley!" My mother's voice bellowed around me like the echoing ring of a large bell, and her hands gripped me from both sides, shaking me and repeating, "Wake up!"

I came to enough to recognize who was screaming. It was not my mother — it was the Mother. She'd come for me in the middle of the night, and I had been caught prone, with no place to hide all the bad I'd done. The Mother pulled me from the bed, dragged me into our small kitchen, pointed one long finger, a beautiful one that sometimes belonged to my real mother, toward the open trash can. I hadn't even tried to bury the cigarettes deeper in the trash bag, they sat right on top, looking back at me, accusing me, and I accepted their blame. I was guilty. I knew this. The garbage knew this. And now, so did the Mother.

I went to sleep sore, but grateful once again that the Mother hadn't lost control. I was hurt, but I would not die.

The sunrise could still be mine. Another day.

The next morning, I awoke to the mother I knew, and we both went about our day like nothing significant had happened the night before. I did not blame the Mother for hurting me. It didn't feel like it wasn't my fault. Sometimes I was bad and sometimes people were bad to me. Either way, the badness belonged where it landed. I wanted to believe this was true. That it was all in my control somehow, or in someone's control. All my fault. All my choice. All mine to have or hide or heal.

I decided to pretend to be good, the kind of good that seemed to be best. The silent kind. For the whole day, through school, after school care, and most of the time home with my family, I did not speak unless spoken to. It worked. My mother said, "You're being such a good girl today!" I smiled and said nothing.

I was so quiet my mother didn't notice my eyes were still open when she drifted off to sleep. She didn't notice me whispering to my shadow to keep myself awake. She didn't feel me lean over our wooden headboard in the early morning light, peel back the burgundy curtain, and greet the sunrise all by myself. The sun had risen for me — for me alone — and turned the sky into the painted milk of a soggy bowl of leftover off-brand Lucky Charms. The soft roses and lavenders went on to burn blood orange on the underbellies of clouds. I told my shadow I wanted to keep the sun. My shadow whispered back the instructions for making a memory. I watched the light of day ascend until it hurt my eyes, then I closed them, and taught myself to remember.

My mother didn't know I could do bad things and still have the sun. She didn't know I could keep my own truth and memories inside. But I knew.

3

Before my teacher showed me the bright pastels of morning light, I made friends with the dark in my grandmother's bedroom. Her soft powders and sweet lotions made the space smell more like a pastry shop than a place to rest. More than once she had to pry her various skincare products from the hands of a grandchild as they licked, bit, or swallowed the expensive contents, enticed by scents too mouthwatering not to be edible. Something about my grandmother's room made me feel protected, and so, it was the only place I didn't mind being alone.

Instead of feeling closed in by the silence, I felt expanded by it, part of it, and it welcomed me unlike anything I'd known so far. When I turned out the light, nobody guessed I was in there telling myself stories, building safe places to go inside my head. They would walk right by me, never knowing I'd been there beside them in the dark.

I don't remember if my grandmother's apartment was unlocked or if I knew where to find a key, but the former is most likely. I didn't turn on the lights when I walked through the door. It helped that there was still a bit of light streaming in from the windows in the kitchen and living room, which were only a few feet apart. I began to sing a song to myself, the theme to my favorite cartoon *The Littl' Bits*. With no one to hear but my shadow, I felt safe to sing the tune without punishment. The last time I let out this song, I'd received a smack in the mouth for the favor. Eventually, the adults would realize I actually hadn't been calling anyone "a little bitch," but poorly singing lyrics from the cartoon theme, as toddlers sometimes do. When they repeated this story, they laughed. But there was no fear of retribution here now, where I spun, still singing, up the stairs to my grandmother's bedroom. I flipped the light switch, and stopped singing.

My grandmother had betrayed me. Or, that's how I felt. Her bedroom was full of toys. A small drum set, a Tonka dump truck, a baby doll, a board game whose name I couldn't read to repeat or save inside a memory. There were a few more piled under the initial set of toys I saw, and even more beneath those. She had all those toys — so many things I wanted — and she hadn't been sharing them with me. With me! After R.C., my grandmother was my best friend. For my mother, she was a second parent since my father was in jail. Even when my mother, brother, and I were alone, our unit felt incomplete without Grandma Billie.

How could she keep this from me? The same woman who'd told my mother, "Sometimes I feel so close to Ashley, it's like I gave birth to her myself." I knew, from hearing the story over and over, my mother had responded, "Well, you didn't."

A distant understanding nudged me, and I knew it was time to leave. I was not supposed to be seeing these toys, even if I didn't know why. I'd hoped to snatch a little time alone and spend it singing, spinning, and whispering to my shadow. Instead, I'd done another bad thing. This would be a secret bad thing too. That way, nobody had to get hurt. Nobody had to tell their secrets.

Weeks later, I'd forgotten all about my grandmother's room, and the treasure it held. The fear of getting found out for being there outweighed any desire to reach out to a grown-up with my follow-up questions. I would forget the toys. I would forget the feelings. I would stop sneaking into places I didn't belong. I didn't want to get into trouble, but that feeling was outweighed by the much closer and nagging fear I'd crossed some door into a place I wouldn't be able to come back from.

The holiday season brought all the distraction I needed. My brother and I would sleep under the Christmas tree lights, eyes closed, watching the backs of our eyelids turn blue, orange, red, and purple, calling out the colors as they appeared to us. At least once, our mother would wrap us in blankets in the back seat of the car with snacks and drinks, and we'd drive off into a snowy night. She wouldn't say where we were going, but inevitably, we would end up heading north.

With the downtown of Fort Wayne nearly abandoned, my mother would weave the car down one-way streets heading west, then east, featuring display after display of historical holiday cheer. Our official tour began at the bread factory, where a mechanical wheel of never-ending sliced bread actually never stopped slicing, and the smell of hot flour, sugar, and yeast entwined itself with Christmas. The factory would be decorated with blinking lights cascading from just below the perpetually spinning bread wheel, to what I assumed was the ground beneath us. We'd pass Santa and his reindeer, bigger than life and all lit up on the side of PNC Bank, and he would wink at me. I knew it was a trick of the light, but I winked back just in case the real Santa might know that I didn't.

The drive was nearly over when we got to the bright green wreath on the plaza, but this was also the spot where my mom would park and let us out. All three of us would jump toward the wreath that was mounted much too high for any person to reach. We didn't think we could reach it either, but it didn't stop us from trying. My mother threw snowballs at us and we retaliated until the green lights of the display reflected in the shimmering melted snow in our hair. As we walked back to the car, my body felt warmer than the cold should have allowed, but inside, I felt a sadness from somewhere before, somewhere I couldn't remember, but was certain I hadn't forgotten.

On Christmas morning, we woke to a tree lousy with gifts, some wrapped, and at least one too big for wrapping. My brother and I jumped out of bed, and raced toward the tree, but I stopped just short of my brother and my mother's feet, waiting for the presents to be handed out, like my mother told us would happen. I stood still, my eyes focusing, unfocusing, and focusing again on what I suddenly recognized as a small drum set. My mother did not notice my hesitation before I slid into the spot below her, beside my brother. As excited as we were for our gifts, she may have been even more anxious for us to tear her careful wrapping asunder, and lay our glad eyes on the material fruits of her labor. My mother handed my brother a box double the size of his head covered in what looked like little hand-drawn Christmas trees and ornaments.

The tree. That was all that had been missing in my grandmother's room. If all those toys had been wrapped and under a tree, they would be just like the presents we were opening now. My secret badness came back to bite, and what it had taken left me sadder than I knew what to do with. In the time it took my brother to rip the tree-patterned paper separating him from his brand-new yellow Tonka dump truck, I realized Santa Claus wasn't real. I'd found this secret place inside to shield my bad self, the part that chose not to tell the truth, but it had never occurred to me everyone might have a secret bad self. A self that didn't tell the truth because it had learned the same lessons I'd learned and knew the quiet and the dark could be good places to hide from screams and slaps.

Something cracked, and now I didn't get to delight in the magic, but instead had to pretend like the adults. I'd done it to myself. In search of my shadow, I'd lost some of my childish wonder, and hadn't realized it was a no-trade deal. I wanted to cry. I started to cry. Then I looked at R.C., his big eyes widening, smiling like the sun itself, turning his new truck in his hands over and over. He looked up at me, expecting me to engage in this joyous moment with as much enthusiasm as we'd shared only moments ago. I threw my arms open, stretching through my fingers, and turned to the best, most happiest part of my life, my brother.

"R.C.! Look! Look what Santa brought us!" I didn't know if this counted as a lie, another bad thing to add to the record I'd already begun to keep of my transgressions, big or small. I knew my brother was happy with his truck, happy believing that Santa thought we were good enough to be worthy of such a rare bounty. For my brother, and myself, I put on a show. I already knew I wasn't that kind of good. In my young mind, I'd already proven it.

4

One day, during a family nap on the couch, wrapped in my mother's and brother's arms and legs, I half woke from a dream and thought I saw a man in the corner of the room. I blinked. Still there.

"Go away," I whispered.

He did not go away. I was afraid of him, and as soon as I realized it, he reached toward me and cut my face.

I woke up with the warmth and pressure of my family's bodies still slumbering around me. The man was gone. A dream. My body flooded with relief, and I rolled over a bit, rearranging for comfort. I felt something sticky on my face. I wiped my cheek with the back of my hand, and felt the small hot line of blood before I saw my stained knuckles. It scared me so much, I closed my eyes and pretended to sleep until my mother awakened. I didn't show her my face, waiting for her to notice instead, which only took seconds after opening her eyes. She said I must have scratched myself in my sleep. She cleaned it, and kissed it, and said it might leave a scar. When I showed it to my grandmother, I told her about the man in my dream, expecting her to soothe me, to tell me dreams weren't real, and nightmares wouldn't always come for me when I closed my eyes.

"Did you speak to him?" she demanded, telling me what I'd seen, or dreamed, I wasn't sure anymore, had probably been a demon.

"No!" I insisted. It came out with all the unnecessary aggression of a child's lie, but her face and tone told me "no" was the only correct answer to her question. The memory of whispering "go away" clung to my consciousness, wrapped in fear.

My grandmother said demons find all kinds of ways to show up in your life, even in your dreams, and that their job was to trick me, and everybody else, into doing something wrong.

"Enemies," she called them. "Don't ever speak to them. That's how they get inside you."

Of course, I had a lot of questions about how this all worked. Demons wanted to trick me into speaking to them so they could get inside me, and do . . . what? And, why me? I was just a kid. That's when she explained that right now, I was practicing being a good woman by being a good girl. However, when I turned twelve years old, every bad or wrong action I made would officially count against me in the eyes of God. She told me that God was watching me, but so were the demons, and they were waiting to see who I would decide to become, following the righteous or unholy breadcrumbs I'd left behind over the first twelve years of my life.

According to my grandmother, when I turned twelve years old, I would have agency. My sins would no longer be a failure on the part of my parents, but an individual choice to eschew God, and please the devil.

"Demons," she said, "if they think you're weak enough, will begin to force you to do things you can't even remember doing."

That's probably why I believed my cousins, when they told me I'd burned down our first apartment. The apartment had burned, that much was true. Baby photos, clothes, and other props in the everyday life of a single mother of two went up in flames, but I don't remember any of that. I remember the story my cousins told me, that I had been touching things I shouldn't have, plugging them in, turning them up, and forgetting about them. They told me everything I loved except my family was now ash and dust, and I accepted the blame. I thought it must have been me. Who else would have spoken to a demon?

We moved into a triplex, where my grandmother lived in the back one-bedroom apartment. Her front door was only three or four feet from our back door, and our little family visited her often. My mother's youngest sister, her husband, and their two children lived in the third apartment, the two-bedroom, above us. We didn't visit them quite as much, but that was mostly because we could all almost always be found at Grandma's. I rolled around with my cousins in the grass behind our shared home at all hours of the day, staring into the sky, trying to make them laugh. We were all happiest together.

My grandmother was the first person I remember asking about my father. I was sitting on her bed while she sat beside me folding clothes and separating her dry-cleaning. She owned so many brightly colored, animal-print, or even sequined dresses that they overflowed from her closet, one or two spilling to the floor each time she tried to make room for new arrivals. Her closet was also full of matching shoes and bags that I'd only ever seen her wear into a church for Sunday service, a holiday concert, wedding, or funeral. According to her, these weren't even her best looks.

"When I was young, whew!" Her eyes would complete a full animated roll from one end of the bedroom to the other. "I'm telling you, when I'd go out to listen to music and dance, I would be Dressed. Down."

In her poorly lit walk-in closet, my budding curiosity blossomed. Shoeboxes were stacked in the corner, but when opened, one might find anything from letters I couldn't read, to never-worn costume jewelry my grandmother would thank me for finding. There were also some filled with old family photographs, and I riffled through them often. It was easy for me to form a picture of my grandmother as a younger woman than she was as she stood before me. Forty-seven years old, she had been divorced twice, raised five girls, and was already Grandma to nine children with the tenth on the way in the apartment directly above her own. I walked over to her closet and pulled my favorite photos from a green shoebox in the corner. I spread them out before me, with a few I hadn't seen displayed so I could ask questions about them. I was always asking questions, and she was one of the few adults who didn't ever tell me to stop.

In one old photo, my grandmother sat on the corner of a bed in what looked to be a hotel room. The same unmistakable gap-toothed smile spread across her face while she leaned back onto the bed, exposing an ample portion of her thigh through a sky-reaching slit in the fitted gown. This one was my second favorite. It had so many things I loved. Grandma. A pretty dress. But the best thing was her hair. My grandmother's Afro was big and round and formed a halo around her beaming face, accented by barely-there arched eyebrows. She liked to look her best, and always had. I'd never found a photo of her looking sloppy, a descriptor she despised in others. To my grandmother, there were few things worse than being sloppy. She saw no excuse for the lack of control, even and especially, in herself. In my mind, my grandmother had come into the world a beautiful woman and had continued to be beautiful because that's what she wanted to do. She chose the right clothes, hairstyles, shoes, and furniture. I don't know how. She just knew.

My grandmother even talked to God the right way. When we went to church together, and the pastor invited the congregation to speak praise unto the Lord, my throat would tighten and my lips would go numb. There were a number of hymns I already knew by heart, but when I tried speaking in tongues on my own, even in the safety of a bathroom with a locked door, I felt embarrassed watching myself in the mirror. My grandmother was not embarrassed. When the pastor called for it, she would break into the same garbled line. I could tell from the others in church that the language was sacred. After one such time I asked her what she was saying when she spoke that way.

"You won't understand," she told me. "It's the way God taught me to speak to him. It's a special language between us. It will never sound right to you."

Once, I pretended to know. After a particularly rowdy and emotional Sunday sermon from her then pastor, my grandmother worked herself up enough to grab my hand and walk us both up to the altar. As I got closer to the pulpit, I could see the pastor touching the foreheads of other church members, praying for them, and then, it seemed, forcefully pushing them to the ground. Ushers, men and women in black clothes and white gloves, rushed to cover the now writhing worshippers with short red blankets. The people on the ground laughed and cried at the same time. I thought they looked silly and a little scary. My grandmother and I stood in line, and when the pastor knocked her to the ground, I wanted to hit him back, but then I heard her laughing. My grandmother, like all the other red worms, wriggled on the ground, filled with the incomparable joy of her holy spirit. When I began to laugh, an usher gently pulled me to the ground beside her, and covered me in a blanket of my own.

I wondered how many people I knew had already learned how to talk with God, and I wondered why God would only give a person one thing to say to him. Wouldn't that get boring? Church was already boring enough. Still, no one else talked about him as much as my grandmother, which caused me to think she must be closest to him. She would know how he preferred to be spoken to. She always knew. Sometimes my mother spoke about God, and so did a few of my aunts and adult family friends, often to tell me how my behavior displeased him. No one else spoke to him the way my grandmother did as far as I knew. But I didn't know all of the grown-ups. We came from such a big family, and had so many close family friends, I felt like I was always meeting someone new who my mother introduced with familiarity and love. Even if I'd never known them before, it felt like I'd forgotten them, and had to be reminded. The photos in my grandmother's closet held numerous stories about family I didn't know, and in some cases would never know. I liked the stories anyway.

I laid the photo of my grandmother in the dress back down on the bed, and picked up one I hadn't seen before. In the bottom of the photo, my brother and I are holding one another in a big hug and smiling toward the camera. Our smiles are big and exaggerated, and I can tell we've been told to put them on. The real joy is in our embrace, while the setting around us is drab. The edges of the backdrop we're standing in front of are rolling up in the corners, and the photographer didn't think or care to cut them out. The floor is made of checkered tile, and the chairs surrounding us are pea green, faded with varying degrees of age and wear. Above us, our mother smiles with her eyes closed into the same camera. She is holding and being held by a man who shares a face with my brother. The man's eyes are happy. I know I'm supposed to know who he is, but I don't.

Without hesitation I turned to my grandmother, held the photo up to her face, and asked, "Who is this man?"

My grandmother stopped sorting her clothes and looked up at the photo. "Girl!" She almost barked the word, the end softening into laughter. She took the photo from my hands and held it closer to her face. Her glasses slipped down the bridge of her nose, landing on the rounded tip. She allowed them to rest there while she scanned the picture, pressing her lips together and shaking her head, until handing the photo back to me. "Damn shame you don't recognize your own daddy."

I can't remember a time before I knew my father was incarcerated, or just "in jail" as I said for the first decade of my life, but I remember a time when he — the fact of his existence — was a hard memory to hold onto. I saw my mother, grandmother, and brother every day. The sun greeted me each morning whether I'd watched it rise or not. I prayed to God each night, like I'd been told. I could count my ABCs, sing along to the radio, and even remember how to tie my shoes if I practiced enough. These things were not hard to remember. But my father, far away, gone without an explanation, would fade away into the background of my four-year-old everyday life until I'd forgotten he'd ever been part of it at all. But before he went to jail, he was here, in a home, with me and my mother. Before he was gone, he loved me.

My grandmother looked around her room like someone might be listening, before sitting down on the bed beside me. I was still staring into the man's face thinking, *Oh yeah. My daddy.* Adults had told me about him before, I was sure, but I hadn't turned those talks into memories. It must not have seemed like useful information at the time. My grandmother leaned toward me and said, "Do you know how much he loved you?"

She sat back on her arms, and looked toward the open door. When she began to speak, the first words came out in a sigh, like she had been holding them in for a long time and was so relieved to finally let them fall away.

"Your daddy took you everywhere. He would have taken you to work if he could have." She laughed a little to herself, and bumped her shoulder into mine like we were old friends. "Your mama would get so mad at him for taking you all over the place, making everybody meet you, and you'd be wearing one sock, and have lines of sour milk stuck between the rolls of that fat neck!" Now, she was reeling, cracking herself up. She made her voice thin and whiny, not at all like my mother's, when she quoted her.

"She'd say, 'Don't be taking my baby out here looking any kind of way!' "

We both laughed at this, both picturing my mother in one of her rages, angry at my father, and protective of how the world saw me. I liked to think of my mother as protective, like she could rage the devil away if he came for me in the night.

"He wanted to show you off any chance he got, and your mama just wanted you to look good while he was doing it. They wanted you so bad and loved you so much. They were just young." She said that last part like an apology, and I didn't understand why.

"When your daddy got locked up, I was in Missouri, and hadn't even heard —" Her mouth shut, eyes closed, and she sat there, silent, remembering or forgetting or trying to say the right thing. "When I got back from Missouri, your mama was waiting on the steps of my house. She was crying, and pregnant with your brother, and rolling around pulling at my skirt going, 'I miss him. Mama, I miss him.' " Grandma wailed a bit as she said this, using every muscle in her face to impress upon me how racked with pain my mother must have been, how much it must have hurt to see her own daughter in that much agony. She looked at her hands.

"I didn't know what was going on. But I told her to get up and come in the house. She was so sad your daddy had to go, and I didn't even know what to say. He had to go. But that doesn't mean he didn't love all of y'all. I know he did."

A swell of gratitude for my grandmother, her photos, and her stories filled my chest. My father loved me, and my mother protected me. But in seconds this memory soured.

I thought of what Grandma had told me once about God. She'd said, "You don't just ask for things when you pray. You pray to say thank you to God, and you pray so he knows you're thinking about the right things." The thought had rocked me. I hadn't known I was supposed to be thinking about specific things that God wanted me to think about. Panicked, I'd asked my grandmother to tell me what each of these "right thoughts" were, so I could be sure to think them. She'd responded as if I weren't a silly child asking a silly question, but someone she was sharing top secret information with. "Just be good and you won't have to worry about it." Then she'd turned and begun to chat with another church grandmother, the kind of conversation I knew it would be disrespectful to interrupt, while my head continued to spin. I hadn't understood why she wouldn't just tell me what God wanted me to do. Now, I wondered if God would be mad I'd forgotten somebody who loved me.

Instead of asking her any more questions, back in her bedroom, surrounded by the images of people who had been important enough to warrant record of at one time or another, I told my grandmother something. "I'm going to pray for my daddy." It seemed a good way not to forget him, by adding his name to my earnest nightly prayers.

"Girl," she said, rising from the bed and gathering the last few unfolded garments in her hand. "God has really touched you." She turned back toward the closet, checked her watch, and told me her friend Wendy was coming to pick her up at any moment. She kissed my forehead and said she needed to start getting ready. "Go play with your brother! He's probably looking for you."

I rushed down the stairs of her apartment, through the kitchen, and out onto the shared back porch. I shut her door behind me, but instead of doing as I'd just been instructed, I hopped down the few steps leading to our backyard, laid on my back in the grass, closed my eyes, and tried to turn my father into a memory. With the sunlight dancing on my eyelids, I pictured my father carrying me from person to person in a crowd, eyes wide, teeth white and beaming, asking each one if they'd had the pleasure of meeting his baby. I pictured my mother admonishing him good-naturedly about the state of my clothes, but glowing with pride because I belonged to her, and I was still a miracle.

The photo I'd found of the four of us would be seared into my memory forever. Our bodies all wrapped around one another's, leaning forward as if we might break into a poorly choreographed tango or waltz at any moment. In the picture, we are frozen this way together, happy, sad, and afraid all at the same time. In the grass, where I made the memory I wanted to keep, we all dance out of the prison doors together, one family, with joy in our smiles and eyes. When we step outside, it is into deep and freshly fallen snow.

5

My mother met a man visiting from Florida, a cousin of someone she knew, and they hit it off. We visited him sometimes. My brother usually stayed behind with one of our aunts, or with Grandma. At four years old, I was more manageable. My brother was young enough to be temperamental and far too clingy. There's a photo of him we passed around as children that I haven't seen in years. In the picture, he sits in the middle of the hallway in our apartment, his small round body leaned all the way to one side, the top of his head nearly touching the ground, keening for comfort or relief as he cries right into the camera. "He wouldn't let me go anywhere!" My mother would pass the photo around, looking frustrated, but also slightly proud. My brother reached for her in a way I did not, and it seemed I was rewarded with more places to go. I knew how to disappear. Sometimes my mother needed me to disappear.

She needed her life back after my father's arrest and this new person seemed like a good way to get it. He was nice enough, though his background with women was messy according to my grandmother. He was always assuring my mother that he was done with someone they only ever seemed to refer to as *her.* Sometimes they would fight about *her.* Once they fought so bad he swung a bag of frozen bread at my mother, missed, and caught me in the face.

There was a sudden burst of confusing pain, then blood shot out of my nose like it was running away from me. It landed on my shirt, and remained there while we all stared. My mother dragged me into the bathroom, sat me on the toilet, and began sticking wads of tissue up my noise. I didn't cry. I was scared that my bloody nose was about to break something between them, and I didn't want my mother to be alone or angry. Plus, I liked him. He was kind to me, and always kept king-size candy bars in the bottom of his refrigerator. I insisted I was fine and it didn't hurt.

My mother was already crying and yelling in the direction of her boyfriend. "Look! Look what you did to my baby!" She continued jamming toilet paper up my nose, and it was starting to hurt. My mother, who only cried like the tears were being ripped from her face, blubbered while she yelled at her boyfriend. Something was happening between her and this man. Maybe something to do with *her.* I didn't know. But I didn't want my mother to cry anymore. I hated it when she cried or yelled. I hated it when she was unhappy. I let her stick tissues into my nose as long as she wanted, and I didn't complain. Her tears told me she was afraid, and I did not want her to be afraid for me.

Standing just outside the bathroom door, her boyfriend buried his face in his palms, then thrust them back into his pockets. He looked sad when he looked at my mother, and even sadder when he looked at me. He crouched down in front of me, took my hand in his, and met my eyes with his own.

"I'm sorry," he said. "I'm so sorry."

"It's okay. I'm okay." He was looking right at me, but it didn't feel like he was speaking to me. I didn't know any adults who apologized to children, and so his apology felt as wrong to me as my mother's tears. I didn't want anyone to have to be sorry to me; I didn't want to make anyone cry. I wanted to make it all stop. "It's okay," I said. "I forgive you." It was the first time I remember saying that to someone. He would come first in the long line of men who would seek to make amends with me. He came before I realized I had the choice not to forgive. Especially when the person offering the apology didn't seem sorry.

It still felt good to be apologized to, no matter who it was meant for. Up until that point, no one had ever apologized for hitting me. I liked the way it made me feel, like I was worth feeling sorry over after someone hurt me, even if they didn't mean it. Like it mattered that I hurt.

My mother never apologized.

Back in one of those memories I'm not supposed to have, I remember being in the kitchen while my mother prepared to relax my hair. I was standing on a stool or chair, as I was not yet tall enough for my head to reach the sink where my hair was being washed. I had been coerced into agreeing to this by smiling adults who'd asked me, "Don't you want pretty hair?" in higher voices than usual. I didn't know what having pretty hair meant, but I liked how their faces lit up when they asked.

Now, my mother hovered over me, the large beautiful hands I would inherit wrapped around my skull, her long and heavy fingers working the relaxer away from my scalp and into the water's stream. I hadn't known the relaxer would hurt. Maybe someone warned me, but by the time it felt like someone had snuck up and set the top of my head on fire, I had forgotten the warning. While fire ants marched across my scalp, my mother tried to push my head under the stainless-steel faucet. My small body hardened with hesitation.

As my head went deeper into the sink, the sound of the water hitting the bottom and splashing onto the sides echoed until it sounded more like the big crashing beach waves I'd only ever seen on TV. The combination of my burning scalp, the pressure from my mother's hands, and the crushing walls of sound coming from the sink caused me to simply freeze. I stood there, burning, dripping, locked up, and refusing to turn my head in either direction my mother requested. She got angry.

My mother grabbed the back of my head with her mighty hand and turned my face into the running water. The water ran into my eyes, and up my nose, and at least a bit of it soothed the edges of my hairline. The watery echo became deafening until it filled my ears, and that's when everything went bad. If I opened my eyes, my mother's face became a blur of a portrait that wouldn't stop melting. I could just barely identify the familiar colors of her skin, hair, and clothing. I considered this may not be my mother at all. When I looked away toward the sink, when I closed my eyes, perhaps there had been a switch. I had no idea who was holding me now. I couldn't see, taste, smell, or hear anything. The water that had gone up my nose was threatening to fall down my throat and become trapped there. Everything I felt, hurt. I couldn't breathe. I opened my mouth to shout, and the stream poured into an airway. I choked, and spit, and finally cleared an airway enough to yell, "Mama!"

I lifted myself from the sink and stared at my mother accusingly. It had been her the whole time. She did not comfort me or apologize. She stared back and said, "Stop being dramatic." I didn't know what that meant either, but I knew I didn't want to be in trouble. More than that, I still wanted pretty hair. Slowly I bent my head back toward the sink, and she began again to finger comb the relaxer from my hair. This time, a bit more gently, and I couldn't deny that it felt good to feel it all wash away. But I stayed tense.

After my hair was rinsed, conditioned, rinsed, shampooed, rinsed, shampooed again, rinsed again, blow dried, greased, and pressed, it was shiny. Dark like my mother's, reaching almost to my shoulders, I looked at myself in the mirror, and I liked what I saw. My hair was pretty. Still, my eyes stung, and water lingered in the canals of my ears. My body was still stiff, and I was already exhausted from the unrelenting tension.

My mother, smiling at me in the mirror, carefully watched my reaction, eager for my approval. Just moments before, she'd turned into an angry stranger with my vulnerable defiant body in her hands. *For that, this is not pretty enough.* I never forgot my mother's face through that curtain of water, warped by the stream, yet clear in its unapologetic expression of rage. It was not a memory I tried to keep.

6

In those days, my mother's moods were more playful more often. She still got mad at my brother and me a lot, but she also played with us, and we loved it when she did.

Our favorite game was something she'd made up called "I'm Not Your Mother." During the game, she would turn off all the lights in the apartment and growl, "I'm. Not. Your. Mother!"

My brother and I would scream, and flail, and run around the room, trying to find a place to hide. Our mother would chase after us, snarling, and swiping at us with her long arms, just missing on purpose, until she finally decided to catch one of us. She'd scoop one of us up and pretend to eat our limbs and faces. It mostly consisted of tickling until we could barely breathe. The game was fun, until the day I took my mother seriously. When she grabbed my brother, and started to "eat" him, he screamed out, "Hashy! Help me!"

For a second, it didn't sound like he was having fun. For a second, I thought I saw the Mother in Mama's face. Something about the tone of his scream was too sharp. She'd lost control. As soon as it entered my head, I ran into the kitchen and grabbed a knife. I sprinted back into the room, held the knife above my head, above my mother, with R.C. still wriggling beneath her.

"Get off my brother!"

My mother, seeing the glint of the knife in the darkness, immediately released my brother, ran for the nearest light switch, and illuminated the room. When she saw me standing there, four years old, and more than ready to mortally wound her for daring to touch the person I loved most in the world, she laughed.

My mother laughed so hard she couldn't stop laughing. Her uncontrollable laughter made my brother and me laugh, so we laughed with her. The three of us fell to the floor, clutched our stomachs, and rolled around with laughter. My mother laughed until she wet herself, and then she laughed harder.

That was the last time we played that game, but there were others.

Every once in a while, my mother, brother, and I would dash around the apartment, checking every couch cushion, corner, and cranny for loose change. My mother had already been keeping a jar of some kind full of pennies, nickels, dimes, and quarters she'd found loose in the bottom of her purse. Though we dipped into that pool of coins every once in a while for a run to Brownlee's Market — where my brother and I would be able to pick out pieces of penny candy from what I assumed were glass jars belonging to Mr. Brownlee himself — the container would still grow heavier and heavier over time.

When my mother told us we were collecting change, that meant we were going to the bank to send our little metal friends down a big spiraling tube that spit out green paper money. Sometimes, my mother would hand me and my brother our own dollar to keep. Even if she didn't, I didn't complain. For me, it was enough to have all gone on this little adventure with one another, and to have watched the magic machine swallow our change and offer us something new in return.

I wanted to be one of those magic machines that spit out real dollar bills, and one day I told my brother we should take the pennies from my mother's stash and eat them. Before we began swallowing copper discs one by one, I hadn't really wondered how many we could ingest. Then once I started, I couldn't stop wondering. I swallowed one after another after another, and my brother kept pace beside me, my truest and most loyal friend, always game to go wherever I led. We ate until we couldn't eat anymore, and then with the fresh and sturdy constitutions of healthy babes, we found another game to play.

About one and a half days later, my brother and I spent so much time alternating going in and out of the bathroom, my mother got suspicious. We were both potty-trained for some time now, but not great flushers, so it wasn't long before we heard a screech coming from the bathroom seconds after one of us had left. My brother and I jumped up and ran to the open door where my mother stood looking down into the toilet in horror. We looked in too, worried one of us had left something in there that wasn't supposed to be flushed like car keys or the head of a doll. But there was just poop. Then I saw what I'd missed in the first scan. It was poop, that couldn't be denied, but it was shiny. The soft ripple of water of the still running toilet caused the copper edges of digested coins to glimmer in the bending light.

"Are you motherfuckers crazy?" Our mother didn't blink, but her voice was so calm, we knew it best to stay quiet as well. "You could have broken my toilet!" She slammed the seat down, and the resounding CLAP made us jump. We waited for the blows, for the Mother to come claim the pound of flesh that was rightfully hers, but instead, she began to laugh. She laughed and laughed and began to ask an imaginary someone out loud, "Whose kids are these?" My brother and I started laughing too, but before we could have too much fun, my mother fell silent again. "If you do this again, it's going to be real trouble. Do you understand me?" We said we did, and backed away from the door as she walked toward us. She made her way back to the couch, shaking her head and giggling.

I was always trying to figure out which version of myself to be to not upset her. I didn't often get it right. I didn't realize I wasn't supposed to know or repeat the things my mother and grandmother gossiped about, until about a year later when a woman had come knocking at the door. She'd previously occupied my aunt and uncle's apartment above us, and my mother and grandmother would whisper about the roaches creeping out of her apartment and into ours, my grandmother insisting at least once that she'd watched one of the bugs make the whole trip from one apartment to the other. When they saw the neighbor, they'd offer one another a look, and sometimes added a single word as an explanation for it: "Drugs."

The knock came again, and my mother told me to go peek through the window and see who it was. I did as she asked, then proceeded to turn and loudly announce to the rest of the room, "It's just the crack-head lady from upstairs."

My mother's anger came swift and sharp across my butt and back. I had no idea what I'd done wrong. The pain rattled in my small body and mind. I was confused. I didn't know how to be the child my mother wanted me to be. Just as quick as her blows came, she erupted in laughter. She would later recount this story to other family members, nearly choking herself as she giggled through it.

"I couldn't believe she said that! I sure did whoop her ass that day." My mother's face would split into the smile I rarely saw. It illuminated her entire face, from hairline to chin. I thought that smile was her prettiest. I didn't mind when she told those stories. I craved seeing her happy, witnessing that smile. It was easier to laugh at the jokes after you'd forgotten the pain. That smile sometimes made me forget the pain, and I would laugh too. Over time, forgetting the pain to make the best joke got easier and easier and easier.

7

My mother wanted to be with her boyfriend. He wanted to be with her too, but there was distance, and youth, and there always seemed to be some other woman involved. It would not last between them. He'd come into her life quickly, and he left the same way. The culmination of the first phase of that relationship, the baby, my second brother, was born without ever breathing. My grandmother said he was born small and gray, with an exposed serpentine spine. When she repeated this story, she would push up her glasses, wrinkle her nose, and use her index finger to make a wavy line in the air to illustrate the curve of his body. She said my mother held him for hours, kissed the top of his head, rocked him against her chest.

My mother hadn't wanted to have another baby, not without being married. But abortion wasn't an option, and he kept growing inside her. My mother could not fathom what kind of good Christian woman would end the life of a child, even if she was in no position to provide for him, and my mother very much wanted to be a good Christian woman. Still, she did not want to be pregnant. And when the baby was born already dead, she blamed her desire to be free for his passing. She named him after his father. She did not mark his grave.

My mother came home to us raw and all alone. My grandmother told me she sat in the bathtub for hours, bleeding into the water. She stared into the space between herself and the walls, her body purging its sin, staining the off-white fiberglass. Her silence worried my brother and me for reasons we couldn't grasp just yet. He and I would sit close enough to hear the water make small splashes when she adjusted herself, making sure she wasn't giving up on breathing or living, that she wasn't giving up on us. On the other side of the door, my mother sent noiseless prayers into her bathwater, repenting in spontaneous expulsions, oblivious to the world growing red around her.

Grandma and my mother's sisters wanted her to be well. They took her back to see the man who had delivered baby Darrell and the hole in his back. They told him my mother's symptoms because she'd lost her voice somewhere down in her chest, somewhere they couldn't reach in and grab it. She'd stopped trying to find her voice days before. She was content in her silence, in her bleeding, and in her inevitable demise. The doctor told my grandmother it was psychosomatic. My grandmother called him a quack and a demon.

He said, "There's no reason for her to be bleeding anymore. She's using her mind to punish herself. She won't get better until she chooses to get better."

Someone decided my brother would stay with my mother, and I would leave with my grandmother. We moved to her father's, my great-grandfather's farmhouse in Columbia, Missouri. A few years later, when I couldn't quite remember the worst of this time, I'd ask why I was sent off with Grandma Billie before kindergarten. I would be told, "Because you said you wanted to go."

I disappeared into a new life in Missouri — a life without either brother, living or dead, and a grandmother who put strawberries and whipped cream on my waffles without blood under her nails. There was no one for me to protect or worry over. I missed my mother, but less and less every day. To keep me company, I had a dog, a goat, and a great-grandfather who threw hammers at wild pigs in the backyard then paid me two dollars to collect the tools and bring them back in the house. It was a game I thought my brother might enjoy, but I tried not to think of my brother too much. When I did, I felt sick with missing him. I couldn't forget him if I tried.

My grandmother and I had our own routine. I had school and day care all week, and I got to see a movie and get one toy on Saturdays. We alternated picking the movies, and when it was my turn, I could pick whichever movie I wanted, all by myself. I was electrified by the power of my choice, and made my decisions based almost exclusively on the posters outside the theater. That's how I ended up picking films like *Lorenzo's Oil, Passion Fish,* and *Groundhog Day.* I was easy to please, and never protested my grandmother's picks, even after *Fire in the Sky* made me cry myself to sleep for a week. My grandmother was loving, but being comforting wasn't her gift. Each night she taught me to read alternating between the Holy Bible, Barbie comics, and supermarket celebrity tabloids. I thought Princess Diana and Mary Magdalene would have looked similar. I thought the same about Billy Ray Cyrus and Jesus. When the thought of alien abduction kept me up, the *Star* magazine I kept under my pillow reminded me to stop holding my breath.

Living with my grandmother and her father in the fields of Missouri, I learned to think only of myself for hours at a time. Spending half a day alone, free of the company of people who would distract me from my being, I learned to think about who I was, who I was becoming, and what I wanted.

I spent my free time exploring my great-grandfather's land, roaming farther than I was allowed. Too young and dumb to be scared of them, I made a game of sneaking up on and catching garden snakes by the tail. I caught them fast enough to shock them, and then dropped them before they caught my skin between their fangs. I was only bitten once. It was fast and painful, but I did not scream. My eyes got wide and my arms flailed around until it let go. After the garden snake released me, I closed my eyes and leaned against a tree. I steadied my breath and soothed myself by speaking directly into the two puncture wounds in my first finger.

"It don't hurt, Ashley." I cradled the stinging hand with its opposite. "If it hurt, you'd die. You won't die."

On our Christmas visit to Indiana, my mother accused my grandmother of turning me against her.

"She acts like she doesn't even know who I am."

My mother's tongue was coated in venom, her familiar anger rising in the back of her throat.

A few days before Christmas, my mother came into the living room and saw me playing with a doll. It was the same doll she'd bought and wrapped for me under the tree. It was a doll she knew I'd love, something she hoped would remind me of the games we used to play, and the life we'd had together back when we lived in the studio apartment. Now she was renting a two-bedroom house with enough room for me to return, but I was still in Missouri. No one thought it would be a good idea for me to move back to Fort Wayne in the middle of a school year. But my mother missed me, and wanted me home.

She screamed at me for opening the present, a gift she had to have worked overtime to purchase. I did not only feel distant from my mother, I felt angry with her, and unsure of what she wanted with me. She sent me away, called me back, and now she seemed mad that I was here. I started to walk away from her and found myself buried face-first in her living room carpet. My mother kicked me. I didn't cry.

After a few moments, my mother picked me up and held me against her. Being held was rare, and precious, an offering in and of itself. I rejected it, making my body go limp. I hoped she thought I was dead or paralyzed. I wanted her to think she'd really hurt me. I wanted her to apologize like her old boyfriend did. My grandmother walked into the room, took a look at us, and asked what happened. My mother told her I'd opened my gift. My grandmother explained that she'd bought me the same doll in Missouri. My grandmother knelt beside me.

"Are you okay, baby?"

I looked toward the front door. "I'm fine. It don't hurt. I'm not dead." My mother walked into her bedroom and shut the door.

"Grandma, tell her it's okay. I'm not dead. I'm alive."

When my grandmother and I returned to the farmhouse, I jumped out of my grandfather's car and ran into the house. I ran into the sitting room where my tea set was always on the back table, then into the bathroom where my good toothbrush was still in the pink cup behind the sink. I touched all the things that reminded me of my new life in Missouri where no one hit me, I could read as much as I wanted, and there were no rusty red stains left in rings around the bathtub. I spoke to my grandmother without looking at her.

"Don't ever make me leave again, okay? I don't want to leave again."

She looked down at me, then into the backyard, into the places I played without permission. She grabbed my hand and walked me out toward the trees, grabbing a shovel and a burlap bag next to the grill on the way. We walked farther and farther back until we were in the part of our land where my great-grandfather let the grasses grow long. My grandmother stomped around a bit, then staked the shovel's blade into the dirt. She dug slowly, and with purpose, like she was sneaking up on the earth spread out before us. The ground was soft so it wasn't long before she told me to come closer.

I leaned over the hole and saw a garden snake. No. Two, three, four . . . a lot of garden snakes. They were in some sort of a knot, though not stuck together. They moved quickly and deliberately over and around one another. They were not fighting, and they did not seem to be trying to get away from us or anything else.

"What are they doing, Grandma?"

My grandmother stared into the hole.

"They're loving each other, baby."

She reached into the bag, poured lighter fluid into the hole, then a lit match. The grass in and around the hole burned, and then, so did the snakes. My first instinct was to reach in and throw them as far as I could, to safety, but I hesitated when I remembered their bite; I waited too long to do them any good.

The snakes did not slither away or thrash around as they burned. They held each other tighter. Even as the scales melted from their bodies, their inclination was to squeeze closer to the other snakes wrapped around them. Their green lengths blackened and bubbled, causing the flesh that simmered underneath each individual metallic hood to ooze. They did not panic, they did not run. I started to cry.

"You will have to go back. We'll both go back home. Your mama misses you." My grandmother reached over and grabbed my hand, both of us still staring into the hole. "These things catch fire without letting each other go. We don't give up on our people.

We don't stop loving them."

She looked into my face, her eyes watering at the bottoms.

"Not even when we're burning alive."

8

When we took the Greyhound bus back to Indiana, my grandmother dressed us in matching hot-pink sweat suits, so we wouldn't lose one another in a crowd. When all the people waiting for the buses got pushed together, especially while boarding or leaving, my grandmother squeezed my fingers in the palm of her hand, holding me close to the side of her body, staring daggers at anyone she felt got too close to me. I hated the hand-holding. I could feel the fear and tension in my grandmother's face travel down her neck and shoulders, into her arm, then into her hand, crushing mine. It made me feel afraid, but there didn't seem to be anything to be afraid of. It made me afraid of whatever I couldn't see coming. But I loved the matching outfits. I was too young to be embarrassed by them, had no need to feel separate from her in our looks, and besides, my grandmother always knew how to dress. I was proud to look like her. Proud to be seen by her, and felt slightly safer knowing she was always watching.

Weeks earlier, she'd told me it was time to go back home, that my mother missed me, but I did not agree. I rested my forehead against the bus window, careful to avoid the red bar warning that this was an emergency exit. One time, on a bus ride before this one, my grandmother told me that if I fell asleep against the bar, I might slip out of the window and into the road before anyone would notice I was gone. As she said it, I could see it — my small sleeping body tumbling from the side of the bus, falling into the traffic, smashed into the road, and all the bus patrons, driver included, continuing toward the Hoosier State, with no real sense that a little girl who had just been real and alive beside them, was now dead and gone behind them. I taught myself to sleep lightly, to feel the difference between the window and the bar on my face. As I tried to sleep now, the light vibration of driving down the highway soothing me, I dreamed of the tea set I'd left behind, and the farm where I could be anything and anywhere I wanted with a little imagination. When I woke again, my grandmother was telling me that my mother had moved into a new place and there would be more room to play — that we would all be starting over again in Indiana.

I did start over in Indiana, but not in the way my grandmother promised. Things were different when I got back. It had been almost a whole year and I came back to a baby sister, Nikki. I'd known about her, but had also kind of forgotten about her. Darrell was her dad, but he wasn't living with us. It was hard then, to remember people you never saw in real life. She'd been born two days before my birthday, and I had no memories of my mother even being pregnant. When my mother brought her home from the hospital, I was still in Missouri. My brother loved her so much he couldn't stop talking to me about her. I thought she was beautiful, prettier than I was or had ever been, which my grandmother confirmed.

My mom hugged me with one arm when I came through the door behind my grandmother. My brother hugged me so hard we fell to the floor. "Show her the playground," my mother told him. There were two slides, two swing sets, and a massive sandbox less than one hundred yards from our front door. We ran to the swings first. When we'd swung as high as we could, we let go of the straps midair, and landed in the pit of soft sand. We smiled at each other, big real smiles, and I forgot anything and anyone else. I followed him to the top of the slide, unable to control the width of my grin, even as my face began to sting, and my belly rolled with excitement. "Watch out for that." He pointed to the corner of the platform we stood on. I leaned down until I could see the object, then reared back once I did. A large earthworm wriggled there in two separate parts. Someone had cut it in half. My brother poked his head over my shoulder, and said, "It's going to die." We turned away, and slid to the bottom, one after the other.

It didn't take long for me to integrate into life in the new apartment. My baby sister was funny, my brother had a Nintendo with two controllers, and my mom decorated my room with a white bed, a white desk (with a matching attached bookshelf), and a long white dresser. There were drawings of Black children with balloons and ice cream hanging on the walls in white frames. In the mornings, we all hustled out of the house together, and at night, we usually all slept in the same room. My sister would sleep in the bed with my mother, and my brother and I would make pallets and sleep on the floor beside them. The television stayed on through the night, and I laid awake late enough to watch *Perfect Strangers, Head of the Class,* and *The Golden Girls.* Life here didn't feel anything like Missouri, but it felt good to be with family. Even when I was the last one to fall asleep.

Starting at a new school didn't worry me. I had been what my teacher and grandmother called "a good reader" in Missouri, and since my mother signed my brother and me up for a book-of-the-month program, I'd been reading everything I could get my hands on for months. When we ran out of new books in our house, or I got bored rereading the ones we had, I walked across the street to Aunt Trina and Uncle Scott's apartment, and read their kids' books. In fact, my aunt caught me reading to my cousins more than once. I overheard her tell my mom, "She does all the voices and everything. She's so good."

I hadn't brought much from the farm, but reminded my grandmother more than once to pack all of my *Little Critter, Berenstain Bears,* and *Frog and Toad* books. Then I made her show me that they were packed before we left. She sparked my lifelong love affair with stories, and once I lived with my mother again, my grandmother encouraged her to let my brother and me spend time at our local library. The library felt too good to be true. All those books, on all those shelves, and I could just pluck them out, one by one, find an empty chair, and read, and read, and read. When I realized nobody would stop me from browsing in the teen and adult sections, that books were a place where my age didn't matter as long as I could read the words in front of me, I found a home for my mind and spirit to take root. My imagination had already taken me on a million wild rides, but here was unlimited adventure. For the rest of my life, I would seek out the library the way some search for the soft light of a chapel in the dark.

When we'd been in Missouri, my kindergarten teacher, Mrs. Adams, had told my grandmother I was special. She said this about all the kids in our class. I know this because she said it directly to us. All the time. While handing our little drawings and practice sheets back she'd stop, look each of us in the eye, and say, "Good job, honey. You are so special." I hadn't actually thought I was special, and still suspected I very much was not, but if she wanted me to be special, I would try. At home, with my grandmother, I read books, and watched TV, and I played with everything. At school,

I tried to figure out how to do or be something special.

We'd come back to Indiana two weeks before my first school year was complete, so they mailed my grades. One day, my grandmother came over to the apartment and handed my mother my last report card. It said I'd passed kindergarten. The next day, we got a rare call from my dad. When my mother handed me the phone, I yelled into the receiver, "I passed kindergarten, Daddy! I passed!"

"I'm so proud of you, baby girl." I could hear his smile, his pride, and I soaked it up. "I've got me a smart child."

I liked my first grade teacher, Mrs. York, and she seemed to like me well enough, even though I struggled to keep quiet when I was supposed to. I had a lot of questions, and even more follow-up questions. Still, I sensed she was more amused by me than annoyed, and so I was not afraid of her. It helped that, in general, her decisions made sense. I appreciated the clarity of rules and routine found in her classroom. When she corrected me, she did so with obvious care, and that counted for a lot with me. Kids can always tell the difference between adults who want to empower them, and adults who want to overpower them. She was the former.

There hadn't been any clue Mrs. York was unhappy with me. At least, I hadn't noticed one in enough time. Sometime between the moment I left the school, and the moment I arrived at my mother's front door, Mrs. York had called her. I didn't know this when I opened the door, and my mother's fists came down on my shoulders, knocking the loose straps of my backpack to the floor. I panicked. I ran into the sitting room next to the kitchen, grabbed a cushion from the wooden couch, and attempted to shield myself from the current incoming attack. "What did I do?!" My mind scanned for something, anything I might have done and forgotten about. Did I hide something? Take something? Break something? I was coming up blank, but it was hard to hang onto a thought while my mother thrashed above me.

She stopped hitting me long enough to yell at me that my teacher had called. Apparently, Mrs. York told my mother I'd been caught saying an inappropriately sexual thing to another student. "You said something about a man having his hands down somebody's pants! Where did you see that? Where did you hear that from?" My head continued to spin, confused, trying to remember saying something like that to anybody.

"No, I didn't!" I said, realizing I was telling the truth. "I didn't say that! Mrs. York is lying!" Of course, she must have been lying, but I couldn't understand why.

My mother sneered at me. "That woman doesn't have any reason to lie about you. You did it. I know you did it." But I hadn't. All through me, I knew it was true that I hadn't said those words to anybody. My mother told me I had to call my best friend — the other student she'd been told I was speaking to — and apologize for my behavior. "Don't you ever let me find out you've been saying sick shit to people at school. If you get kicked out, you can't stay here!" I climbed the stairs to my mother's bedroom, and used her phone to call my friend.

"What did you say to me?" she asked. "Why are you in trouble?"

I knew my mother was listening on the second phone downstairs, and I wasn't sure how much I could say, so I just repeated myself, still sobbing. "I'm sorry for the thing I said to you at school today. I won't ever do it again." I could tell she was still confused when she told me it was okay, that she didn't even remember what I'd apparently said. I heard the click as my mother hung up. I told my friend I'd see her tomorrow, and hung up my phone as well. I walked to my bedroom, sat on the bed, and watched the door. *She'll come in,* I thought. *She'll come in, and she'll tell me she's sorry.* I slept in my own room that night, alone, but I woke up on fire.

The next day, I straightened my back as I walked into the school, down the hall, and into my classroom. I put my things away along with the rest of my classmates. My best friend tried to catch my eye, but I avoided her. I had not done what I was accused of, but all the same, I felt ashamed of the accusation. I could hear my mother's voice, drawing out the word *sick* to describe me and what she'd been told I'd done. That word in that tone, landed on and stuck to me. I was certain all you had to do was look at me to see it, so I didn't want someone I cared about to look at me. I wasn't sure I cared about Mrs. York anymore. She'd lied about me.

After finishing my morning practice sheet, busy work I hated, I calmly walked back to Mrs. York's desk. I stood in front of her until she looked up from the papers she was writing on. She looked surprised to find me there, and I was angry about that. She'd called my home and lied about me. My mother had gotten so angry she hadn't spoken to me for the rest of the evening. This woman had no idea the havoc she'd let loose in my home, or what it had cost me. *Or,* I thought, *she just doesn't care.* I felt my anger rise with my breath. *She should have expected me.*

"Can I help you, Ashley Ford?"

I looked into her eyes, and asked, "Why did you tell my mother I said a bad thing when I didn't?" The curious smile dropped from her face, replaced by a confused one. She started to speak, to explain, I think, then stopped herself. She called another student over, a girl, smaller than me who I didn't really know yet. I'd met my best friend, Jamie, on the second day of school and hadn't really branched out since then. One good friend was enough for me. Others would come eventually, but as long as I had one, I felt a satisfactory sense of companionship. This girl was not my friend.

Mrs. York crouched in front of her. "Honey, didn't you tell me you heard Ashley Ford say . . . something yesterday?"

The girl looked at her, then looked at me. Back to her. Again to me. Then she shrugged, and said as if we were both wasting her time, "Well, it did *sound* like Ashley Ford."

This time, Mrs. York's smile faded altogether. "You didn't actually see her say it?"

The girl rolled her eyes. "It did *sound* like her though."

"Okay." Mrs. York raised one hand to stop the girl from speaking, and put the other over her own face. "Oh dear." She looked at me, and understood something unintended had occurred here. And to her credit, she tried to fix it.

"Ashley, I'm so sorry." I believed her apology, and was certain she'd been misled, but knew that wasn't enough.

"You have to call my mother," I said. "Please, you have to call my mother and tell her I didn't say it." She promised me she would. I reminded her again before the end of the day. "You have to tell her it wasn't me," I repeated.

On the bus ride home, I fantasized of arriving to an open door, my mother waiting in the frame, waiting to scoop me up into hugs, and kisses, and apologies. She would tell me how sorry she was, that she should have believed me, that she knew I was good, and she would promise never to hit me again. My mind wouldn't let me imagine much further than that, but that part seemed key, appropriate even given the severity of response the night before. She would want to make it up to me, make it right. That's what you did for somebody you loved, right? At least, that's what you did in the movies.

The door was closed when I walked up to it, but that wasn't the most important part of my fantasy scenario anyway. I opened the door, and walked into the kitchen. My mother was cooking something on the stovetop. I tried to read her body language before approaching, but couldn't detect any specific note of danger. She looked at me over her shoulder, still using her hands to stir whatever was in the pot. "You got homework?" I pulled off my backpack without taking my eyes off her.

"Just reading," I said. We both knew that meant I'd already finished. "Did my teacher call you?"

She stopped stirring the pot. "Yes, she did."

She started stirring again. I took a step closer to her back, unsure if she had heard me, or if we were talking about the same call. "Did she tell you that I didn't say that thing? Did she tell you that girl lied on me?"

My mother stopped stirring the pot again,

and cut off the burner. She turned to face me. Her face was stony and set. We made eye contact, and it scared me, but I didn't feel I was allowed to look away.

"Yes, Ashley, she told me. Now why are you still in my face?" She knew what I wanted, and she wanted me to know it would not be mine. We were locked in a power struggle, not that I would have known to call it that, and I was confused because I did not want power from my mother. I wanted her to acknowledge the pain in my body and heart. I wanted it to mean something to her because she loved me, and I knew it, and I couldn't understand why she couldn't just say sorry. What was so wrong with me that I didn't deserve that?

That night, I dreamed I flew across a black night, like the children in *Tar Beach,* to the farm in Missouri, and that when I landed, I saw I'd been cut in two parts, and somehow left one half of myself behind in Indiana. I didn't want to go back for that part.

9

When my brother and I got in trouble, which we did from time to time, and my mother decided we deserved a whupping, he would run. The minute he understood what was about to go down, his feet would start flying. He used to tell me he could tell she was angry before I did, that he saw the signs I couldn't. "If you look close," he whispered to me, "Right before she yells, the hair on the back of her neck curls up. That's when I run!" He would be up the stairs, under the bed, and tucked into a corner too far for her to reach before my mother ever saw him leave. But I would still be standing there in front of her, crying. To me, it didn't make sense to run. The time it saved in anticipation, you paid in pain. I didn't tell on myself, but I always felt caught anyway.

Right before I started the second grade, my mother's work schedule changed. Her new hours didn't permit her to be home by the time my brother and I returned from school, so we stayed with a babysitter. She was a younger woman who lived in the same apartment complex. She'd been hired by a different family to watch their two boys, in their apartment, so my brother and I met them there every day. I didn't like it there, and I didn't like our babysitter. When one of the boys discovered black garbage bags full of porn magazines, he snuck them in a few at a time, and brought them to the rest of us playing video games in a bedroom upstairs. When the babysitter caught us going through one, she sat on the bed and looked at it with us. Everybody else looked relieved, but the pit of my stomach wrenched itself into a ball, and I only felt an increase in danger that now outweighed my curiosity about naked bodies. She made us promise not to tell our parents.

Sometimes my mother would come pick us up from the apartment after work, especially if we would immediately be running an errand or visiting someone. Other times she would call for us, and the babysitter would send us down the sidewalk toward our own front door. After one such call, we gathered our backpacks, and two minutes later walked into a house full of family. It wasn't uncommon to come home to my mother's sisters, their husbands, a few extended family members, and one or two friends of the family lounging around, talking, laughing, and smoking. My grandmother used to say, "What's the point of living by everybody if you don't want to see anybody?" I came from social people, and though I felt overwhelmed by their company, I was always glad to see them. My mother was often in a good mood when she had good company.

Before anyone spoke to me, I felt a difference in this gathering. There was smoking, and talking, but no laughing. The grownups weren't spread out around the house, but huddled in the small living room. My brother and I began to walk slowly and only on the balls of our feet, afraid of making any unintended noise. One of my aunts said, "How could she not believe her own baby?"

The rest began to answer all at the same time, "Over a man."

"That girl said he touched her!"

"Couldn't be me!"

"I would die first." That was my mother. "I would die before I let anybody hurt my kids."

She looked up then, and saw my brother

and me standing in the hallway, halfway between where she sat and the door we'd just walked through. "Upstairs," she said. "Go play."

Through a combination of eavesdropping and talking with my cousins, I found out that one of us had accused her stepdad of molesting her. Her mother did not believe her. But we were on my cousin's side. It was an explanation cobbled together by the words of children, and the silence of adults. My mother never told me what happened, not specifically, but our home shifted again. I was seven years old and it had become very important to her that I understood what sex was, and what it meant if someone was trying to do it to me. Over and over she explained to my brother and me that we had sexual parts, but they were private, not to be seen, noticed, or mentioned by anyone else until we were married. "If anybody ever tries anything with you, I will kill them." She'd stare as if we were already hiding something she would soon find out with or without our confessions. "I will believe you, and I will kill them."

My brother and I both had to sit through talks on sex, but only I had to go through the interrogations. My mother became hypervigilant about how I interacted with boys and men, even my own uncles and cousins. She wanted me to see danger everywhere. My mother and grandmother would shake their heads at me and lament that I was too friendly, and that men and boys would take that the wrong way. My grandmother would say, "All that smiling will get you in trouble if the wrong person thinks it's cute."

I didn't want to be suspicious. I didn't want to look at my uncles, cousins, classmates, and teachers and think about what they might be thinking they want to do me. It made me feel sick inside, like I was doing something wrong. Not just bad, which could be harmless, but wrong. Wrong hurt people, and I didn't want to get hurt, or hurt anyone else. I still didn't understand how fear like my mother's would protect me. In truth, it wouldn't. It never could.

My mother insisted I learn to be more skeptical, and my lapses in judgement infuriated her. When my twelve-year-old cousin, T, brought one of his guy friends over, I didn't give either of them much of a second thought. When they started talking about buying candy from the lady who sold it in paper brown bags out of her unit across the parking lot, I perked up. I had five one-dollar bills and three quarters in my top dresser drawer. I gave them two quarters so they had enough to get a full bag. T lifted me up in the air, and kissed me on the cheek. "Thank you, Ash!" They both left, money in hand, sprinting down the parking lot.

"What was he thanking you for?" My mother came out of the kitchen, and stepped into the hallway between me and the door. I considered lying for no other reason than she already looked mad. I didn't.

"I gave them fifty cents so they could go see the candy lady." I couldn't see how that could be bad, but my stomach already hurt as I explained it. Something about it was wrong, I just didn't know what yet.

My mother got down into my face, and I thought she would hit me, but she didn't. She spoke to me through her teeth, her eyes wide and fixed on mine, daring me to blink in any way that could be misinterpreted. "Don't. Ever. Give. A. Man. Your. Money." A man? T? His friend? It didn't matter. I nodded okay, lied that I understood.

A few months later, I came home from a sleepover at a friend's house, and as soon as I walked through the door, my mother grabbed the bag of clothes I'd taken with me. She asked me how it had gone, and I began to list everything we'd done from bike-riding to movie-watching, then I noticed she was going through the bag, looking for something. She held up a piece of cloth, looking confused and then angry. She turned to me, and I stopped talking. She thrust a pair of dirty underwear into my face, and asked, "What is this?" I couldn't see anything. She never actually stopped shaking the underwear as she asked me to identify what was in them before she asked again, "Ashley, what *is* this? Why does this look like blood?" My body went cold and still. No sudden movements.

I spoke because I was afraid my silence would say untrue things. "It's just vagina goop, Mama." That's what I'd been told to call it the first time I found something in my underwear that wasn't pee, and hadn't been there before. Those were the right words, right?

I trusted my mother to deliver the violence she'd promised upon anyone she believed violated something that belonged to her. She explained it was her job to protect me from those sick people, and so it was important for me to tell her the truth, so she could do her job. But telling the truth wasn't enough. I had to make her believe me with my voice, and my body, and my face, which always seemed to be doing the wrong thing in those moments. I thought, if I can't make her believe me, somebody could die. Somebody could die because my mother refused to believe I'm not a liar, and I couldn't convince her otherwise.

10

My mother called me at the Boys & Girls Club to tell me Grandpa would be picking me up, which he did from time to time to help her out. Usually, I loved that call. It meant I'd get to stop at McDonald's on the way home, and he'd let me order my own large value meal. But after we scooped up our fast food, Grandpa told me my mother would be a little late, and we were going to hang out at his house. I fixed my face to hide my disappointment. He didn't have cable, and instead of *Punky Brewster,* I'd most likely end up watching him.

Grandpa sat at the table, sorting the edible parts of an almost-dead frog. His fingers bent and popped its sinewy limbs, separating the muscle from bone. The nearly departed performed a table dance for me. I was unimpressed. I wanted to be anywhere else in the world.

The kitchen walls were smoker's teeth.

Age and negligence caused them to sweat a yellow film. I stared at them, doing my best to ignore the small splashing sound coming from an old white bucket next to the refrigerator. He'd caught a catfish earlier the same day. It had not wanted to be caught. My grandpa started talking to me.

"Don't trust them boys out there, little girl. They ain't worth shit, and they don't know shit." He spat the words onto the twitching frog's half-open body. If it had been even a little more alive, I wouldn't have been certain he was speaking to me. I nodded. Nodding was always the right answer, even when no one asked you a question, and especially when you hadn't really been listening. My grandpa loved to tell me stories about his past exploits, his current exploits, and the exploits he planned on having in the future. I was not afraid of him, but his wild tales made me uncomfortable, so when I could, I tuned him out. I wasn't allowed to say that because it might hurt his feelings. But it was true.

It was clear that he didn't really know what to do with children or what was appropriate for them to watch, see, or hear. How would he know? Though he'd lived in the same city as his children, he hadn't had much to do with the upbringing of any of his four daughters with my grandmother.

"You think you got it so bad with your daddy being away?" my mother once said to me. "Your dad wishes he was around. He'd give anything to go back in time so he could be here with his family. My dad didn't live five miles away, and I didn't see or speak to him for weeks and months at a time. I didn't even know if he cared."

My grandfather had only recently attempted to become a more consistent part of his daughters' lives. We would all go out to a lake as a family, and my grandpa would teach all of us how to fish or catch frogs. Sometimes, the grandkids would run off into the woods or fields near wherever we were playing hide-and-seek. My mother and her sisters would stand around with their father, talking and laughing. Despite his absence in their childhood, they all seemed to enjoy his company enough now. Even my grandmother would sometimes have him over to watch boxing. He was the only person she knew who enjoyed it just as much as she did. He even started to have his grandkids, like me, over sometimes just to hang out. We were all getting used to him.

It never occurred to Grandpa it might be a little too much for a kid to watch him cut up living frogs, or that I might have been too young to sit on the couch and watch *From Dusk till Dawn* in the middle of the day as if it were a family film. He was doing his best, what he knew how to do. I was usually happy to spend time with him, but more and more, I just wanted to be home. I wanted to be with my mother and brother and sister. I wanted to watch TV in my bedroom, and read, and draw, and be surrounded only by things I could anticipate. Ever since I learned my cousin's secret, a secret she kept but hadn't chosen, I lost something that made me feel generally okay. It was replaced by the steady drum of fear that made my heart race and my stomach drop. That feeling happened less when I was home, and so I almost always wanted to be home. I was desperately trying to feel generally okay again.

School had been a safe place for me, until my teacher suggested that my advanced reading level required me to be moved into a second/third grade split classroom. My new teacher seemed nice enough, but a few of my classmates didn't like me almost immediately, which was fine. Though I spent a significant amount of time trying to figure out the best way to be good, I didn't spend much time at all, outside of with my immediate family, trying to be liked. Some people liked me, and some people didn't, and that seemed okay. Until one boy, Ty Applegate, zeroed in on me as a target. He lived in my apartment complex, he was a lot bigger than me, and he beat me up every time he saw me playing alone, as I preferred to do. Eventually, my mother told me if I didn't hit him back, then she would hit me for not protecting myself. The next time I saw A. J., I threw a rock at his mouth before he could hit me. He fell to the ground, screaming in pain, and I seized my chance to hit and hit and hit and hit. As I attempted to drive this boy into the sandpit beneath his writhing body, I remembered my grandmother telling me, "I never lost a fight in my life, because I never stopped fighting until I won."

Grandpa didn't have to tell me not to trust boys. I already knew I couldn't. And men. Especially men. At that point in my life, Grandpa was one of the only adult men who didn't make me nervous. Even my uncles, who had never done or said anything to make me question them, caused me to feel nauseous at the thought of being alone in a room with them. That was because of what had happened to my cousin. Ever since I found out that her stepdad had touched her, I hadn't felt right around most boys, and any men at all. The fear that bloomed in my center was foreign to me, unlike any I'd ever felt before. It was the kind of fear that made you cry before anything even happened. And I did. I started crying myself to sleep again. I didn't tell my mother that. Nothing pissed her off more than my tears, and I couldn't see how these would be received any differently from the ones that came before.

My mother had become obsessed with making sure that what happened to B wouldn't also happen to me. Whenever I went to someone else's home to play or spend the night or anything, my mother would grill me as soon as I walked back into her house.

"Who was there? Did something happen to you? Did anybody touch you? You better not lie to me!" My mother's face would stare down at me angrily as if I had done something wrong, as if she knew the truth and was just waiting for me to confess. Her words terrified me. I became afraid such an event was inevitable. Why else would my mother be so insistent I not lie to her about these things? Why else would she seem so mad at me? I wasn't sure I could protect myself physically if someone did try to touch my body, and so I thought it best to hole up in my bedroom. Hadn't that been what my mother was trying to teach me? That being touched could happen at any time with any man? Even if I hated the way she spoke about these things, I was made properly afraid by her warnings. Protecting my body became my number one goal. My grandpa didn't have to convince me that was necessary. If a man spoke to me while I was alone, I cowered in fear. I tried to see them all coming, because in my child mind, they were all coming for me.

Grandpa told me stories that would get hung up old, useless, and dry against my ribs, marking me as his kin. My brother and grandmother were the only ones ever interested in anything Grandpa had to say. My brother wanted the laughs. My grandmother wanted confirmation she had done the right thing by walking out on him decades earlier.

I knew he used to hit my grandmother and that she used to hit him right back. I knew I wasn't supposed to talk about that. If I closed my eyes when he told his version of some old story, I pictured my grandmother wielding a cast-iron skillet in one hand, a pot of boiling water in the other. I saw Grandpa running away from the water only to be bludgeoned by eight pounds of Calphalon weaponry. I thought of my mother in her room sleeping through the noise, or maybe huddled against her sisters, all of them afraid, but for whom? Their mother? Their father? That the house would come falling down on all their heads? Questions I couldn't ask about stories I wasn't supposed to hear.

"She'd knock me on my ass then yell at me for making too much noise." Grandpa let out a small laugh and flung another leg into the pile. His fingers were strong and quick. The frogs seemed to appreciate this about his process. He whipped a frog's torso through the kitchen window, out into his backyard, and chuckled again. I laughed but didn't get the joke. I rarely did. But I knew he liked me better when I laughed.

Just then, the white splashing bucket in the corner turned itself over. Its gaping maw fed the floor lake water and the one live catfish. The water raced toward dirt-filled crannies, places no one else could reach, or no one else had tried. Grandpa and I watched the catfish struggle for oxygen, spastically flipping from side to side, end to end. When it stopped moving, gills still fluttering, Grandpa picked it up with both hands and slapped it down on the table in front of me.

"I wasn't no good. Men ain't really no good." When he worked with his hands, he muttered to himself this way. Mostly about his regrets. He bent the fish into itself until there was an audible pop. I continued to hear the phantom splash from the bucket lying on its side. I couldn't get the sound out of my head even though the fish lay broken before me, and the water was beginning to pool around the bottoms of my feet.

"You'll learn to gut a fish like a man. Then, you won't need one."

I looked up at my Grandpa and felt angry with him. These frogs and fish had eyes, and as far as I knew, ears. Why did I have to listen to his rambling? I thought Grandpa broke and ate everything that might love him. I didn't want to sit here and learn to do the same. But I was already here, gutting a fish like a man as if I knew what that meant. And it was another thing I had to know, and not repeat. I would always know how to gut a catfish in a frog's grave. I was sewn into his regrets. I would always be at least a little angry.

When Grandpa laced his fingers and turned his elbows out, ready to release tension and air built up between his knuckles, I covered my ears with scale-stained hands. I begged him, "Please, don't." He stopped and stared at me, startled by my voice. I thought the sound his hands made would hurt me. It would be too loud, and too sharp. I couldn't explain why I knew that. I just did. I was the fish on the table between us, pushed into myself so hard I would soon snap in half. The feeling started in my hand and creeped out into my already shifting body. I was not safe. Nothing about me was safe from drowning in the open air. It was my first panic attack. My grandpa watched it happen until it was over, then he drove me home.

11

It was a party, New Year's Eve, and my mother's apartment was full of aunts, uncles, cousins, and family friends. The kitchen was where conversation came to a boil, bubbling over the top until someone had the good sense to bring the temperature down with a good joke. I listened from various corners of the room. Each face was familiar, but the energy was different. Parents were different when their children slept, and I had become an expert at making myself invisible enough to watch the transformation.

My mother's smile was so wide, the laughter fell from her mouth in a slant. I loved watching her like this. She looked warm and happy. My mother was made for a good party, but rarely got to indulge in them. She never complained to her kids about it, but I knew. Our apartment was small, and her voice was big — I knew she was alone and not happy about the fact. Sure, she was dating someone, but she wasn't married. There was no man to split bills with, co-parent with, or dream about the future with. In that sense, she was lonely. But tonight, she was alive. She was surrounded by her family.

"When it comes to family, all we have is each other," she would say to my brother and me often. Especially when we fought. She deserved more. This New Year's Eve she looked like a woman who had more, whether that was true or not.

I watched her quietly from across the table. The easiest way for a child to lose their seat at the adult table is to speak. If no one hears your voice for long enough, they forget you're there. They let things slip. They say things they wouldn't normally say in front of a child. Even the adults who notice and remember you're present will simply point a finger in your direction and make direct eye contact.

"You better not repeat any of this, you hear?"

I had no interest in repeating anything I heard. I was much more interested in bearing witness to all this freedom. Grown-ups seemed lighter at night, like their feet might hover an inch or two off the ground as soon as the sun went down. The later it got, the higher they flew. It didn't make me want to grow up faster; I was content to wait my turn. Even then, my childhood seemed precious and like something to cling to. I just wanted to watch and be awed.

My mother and her sisters were all either married or dating, or at least, I thought so. At this party, there was one male family friend who wasn't around often, but I knew him. He was always smiling and slipping dollar bills to us kids. He was about as old as our uncles, but he actually spoke to us, and didn't seem annoyed by our presence. As good as I was at being invisible, there was nothing I liked more than being spoken to like an adult. When he noticed me sitting quietly on the couch way past my bedtime, he caught my eye and winked. I smiled and waved back, happy to be noticed without being dismissed.

Right before midnight, the grown-ups felt free to get rowdy. Their eyes were wild. I was still invisible, but now they seemed to even stop seeing each other. They laughed so hard they bumped into one another. They knocked over plastic cups, and sloppily cleaned up their messes with handfuls of paper towels. Eventually, someone turned on the TV so they wouldn't miss the countdown. Someone else almost knocked the TV over. I went into our dark living room to sit by myself for a while and calm down the inside of my head. The adults with the wild eyes made me nervous. I leaned against the patio door, trying to leave small handprints on the cold glass, just something to amuse myself.

"What you doing in here by yourself?"

This man, this family friend, was so nice, his voice didn't even startle me. I didn't answer, but started making more handprints all over the glass. I looked back at him and raised my eyebrows.

"See?"

He walked over, knelt beside me, and started making handprints too. It occurred to me that my mother might not appreciate handprints all over her patio door, but if a grown-up was doing it with me, I figured it couldn't be all bad. Grown-ups, in general, knew how to not get in trouble with other grown-ups. I assumed that was why they didn't yell at or hit one another as much as they yelled at and hit children. I trusted him to know if the handprints were going to get us in trouble. I trusted him.

Noise from the kitchen swelled as the clock ticked closer to twelve. He turned to me with wide excited eyes.

"Ashley, it's almost midnight. It's going to be a whole new year. What do you think about that?" I considered his question. I wasn't sure what happened at midnight on New Year's Eve. I'd never stayed up late enough to properly watch one year pass into another. Besides, I hadn't stayed awake to see what would happen, I'd stayed awake to watch what was already happening. I turned to him.

"I think it's good."

"It is good. Do you know what happens at midnight?" I shook my head.

"At midnight, you kiss someone you love. Do you love me?" Another question to consider. He was nice and he was like family. Family was all we had. To me, that was enough to love. I nodded.

"Yeah, I love you."

He suggested we countdown together, and I thought that sounded fun. We held up both our hands in front of our faces, and chanted along to the numbers we couldn't see, folding one finger into our palms for every number spoken aloud.

10

9

8

7

6
5
4
3
2
1

My mother's apartment exploded with celebration. I quickly covered my ears to save them from the initial burst of noise. He got close to my face and I pushed out my lips. Then the back of my head hit the patio door.

I could feel the cold glass on my scalp while he used the force of his tongue to drive my lips apart and invade my mouth. His shaking hands were on either side of my head, and while my eyes were wide open, his were screwed shut. I thought I'd seen a kiss like this in a movie once, but it had looked nice. This was not nice. It did not feel nice. I felt trapped, and tricked, and wrong. In a moment I'd been flung into a new and clear understanding: my grandmother and mother's fear had been correct. Danger was everywhere.

Someone called his name from the kitchen and he scrambled away from me like I'd bitten his tongue. I was glad. I wished I had bitten his tongue. I wanted to be able to tell my mother I had bitten his tongue. Now, I wouldn't be able to. After a moment, I peeled myself away from the glass and walked past the kitchen. The grown-ups were all back on the soles of their feet. There was no more floating, at least none that I could see. I found the only face I still cared to see glowing.

"Mama!" I rushed over to her. My mother looked down at me, confused.

"Why are you still up? Ashley, you think you grown. Go to bed. Now."

Arguing was pointless. She was right, I should be in bed. I'd made myself visible, and that was the wrong thing to do. I headed up the stairs to my brother's room. I was older, but that was where I slept when I was scared. And I was scared.

I looked over to the kitchen one more time, ready to run back and plead with my mother to listen to me. Tomorrow would be too late. Tomorrow I would be asked why I didn't say something right away. Tomorrow I would be in worse trouble. I had to tell her what I did before she found out on her own.

Then he stepped into my line of vision.

"Happy New Year, Ashley." He winked. I did not wave.

I climbed the stairs with my hands and

feet and decided to forget about tomorrow, about telling her. Even if I was afraid, he was like family. And all we had was each other.

12

Allen and my mother were friends first. I'm not sure when it became romantic, but I remember when he started coming around. He was pretty normal in the beginning, nice even. But as he and my mother spent more time together, his misery, and need for others around him to join him in that misery, became more apparent. At one time, I thought they might get married. I maybe even hoped for it. Marriage was something my mother wanted. She wanted the whole family, had it once before my dad went to prison. Allen worked, he wasn't sloppy, and he kept coming around. Maybe he was other good things too. I wouldn't have any idea.

His relationship with my mother was off-and-on, and when it was off, she was happier. She dreamed bigger, and wanted more. We would pick up real estate magazines in the vestibules of grocery store entrances, take them home, lie on her bed, and circle our favorites. My mother would task my brother and me with finding our dream homes and sharing them. To me, we didn't need Allen, or any other man. We were already a family. We just needed the house.

"We're not going to stay here," my mother said, waving at our apartment walls. "We're going someplace else." On the weekends, we drove to the houses we'd circled in those magazines, to neighborhoods we couldn't afford to live in, and slowly rolled past their OPEN HOUSE signs, gawking at homes with big bay windows, white columns, and three-car garages. We didn't dare go inside. We didn't dare take a real step toward the physical manifestation of our family dream.

The dream did come true, but it included the continued presence of Allen. I never thought about how my mother bought her house, how she paid the bills, or how she would continue to do so on her own. That isn't the kind of thing a small child would usually be asked to consider. With Allen, it felt like we were on our way home, with a hitchhiker in the back, and the only person who trusted him was the driver.

Still, the first night in the new house was magical. The memories of a day spent watching grown-ups move heavy boxes and furniture into the formerly bare rooms and empty garage of our home have long ago faded, but not the night. I don't remember Allen being there, but instead of wondering why my mother's boyfriend wasn't helping her move, I thanked God for answering my prayers, and hoped as hard as I could that whatever spell kept him away would hold. I hoped that here, nothing bad would find me.

Though the house was newly ours, it was not at all unfamiliar to us. It had belonged to our aunt Terrie, our mother's oldest sister, and she had lived there with her two children, my cousins Tavy and Shira, until she'd gotten remarried to my new uncle, Tyrone. Long before her family moved out of the ranch house, I'd thought it was perfect. It had three bedrooms, and a sizable backyard. The kitchen seemed so big compared to the small one in our apartment. There were monkey bars and a slide in the backyard that were getting a little old and rusty but still provided the same amount of fun they always had when we visited for birthdays, BBQs, and sleepovers. My favorite part was the sunporch that led into the backyard.

The day may have been like any other day, only heightened by the excitement for the potential of a new beginning that trembled in me, but the evening played out like a very special episode of a beloved family sitcom. My mother had had enough foresight to consider she might not want to unpack all evening, so she placed the mattress from her bed in the center of our family room. She put a small TV stand in front of it, put a TV on top, and attached a VCR. Then she turned to me, my sister, and my brother, and told us we were going to pick up a pizza and rent a movie at Blockbuster. All three of us jumped up, always ready for food, especially pizza, and even more ready to fight over which movie we'd pick. Depending on whether or not the video store was running a special, and how new the movies were we wanted to see, we could usually walk away with between one and three movies. I didn't want to ask God for more than I'd already gotten, afraid to seem greedy or annoying, but I wanted one more thing, so I prayed:

Please let it be a three-movie night.

My mother called Pizza Hut about ten minutes before we left the house for Southgate Plaza. Southgate was the shopping center, slightly closer to our house than Southtown Mall. Grandma and I often rode the bus there, stopping in almost all of the stores and shops to browse, usually buying nothing. The only place she and I rarely stopped, but my mother always took me, was Blockbuster. My grandmother didn't care for watching movies on VHS, she preferred the big screen. But I loved them, and so did my mother. Renting and watching a movie together felt sacred, and for her, I think the same was true. She paid attention to my tastes, and at times, catered to them. When one of my aunts asked to borrow *The Joy Luck Club,* my mother stopped her and said, "Ashley hasn't seen it yet, and I think she'll really like it." She was right, but I wasn't even ten years old.

My mother entered the Pizza Hut parking lot, and quickly found an empty spot. She turned to all three us, strapped into the backseat of the wide sedan, and fixed us there with her eyes.

"I'm going in here to pick up this pizza," she started, her eyes settling on each of us before moving on to the next. "When I come back out here, y'all better not have moved nothing, touched nothing, or gotten out of this car. Do. You. Understand." The last three words were punctuated by another hard stare at each of us, a singular warning that counted the same for one and all. The warning was necessary. More than once, my mother had come out of a store only to find my brother or me sitting in the driver's seat, pretending to drive, and screaming some song on the radio at the tops of our lungs.

Not this time. Nobody was going to mess up pizza and the potential for a three-movie night. Not me. When my mother left the car, we sat and sang to ourselves. Our cars sometimes had cassette players, and sometimes didn't, but they always had the radio. There was nothing like Anita Baker suddenly crooning from the dash, *I apologize / Oh believe me I do / I apologize / Oh honest and true . . .* The way my mother would reach for the volume to turn the song up, like a lottery winner who'd just heard the DJ call out the last of her lucky numbers lit a spark in me. If she was smoking a cigarette, she would roll down the windows and sing into the wind, one hand on the wheel, and the other dancing to the music. While she held down the front of the car, her children responded in chorus until we were all howling with heartbreak. *Because I know I was wrong / So I'll sing you this song / Cause I wanna get through / And make it up to you.*

My mother loved music. She doesn't play any instruments, but she sings well, and she's been singing to me my entire life. She would fall in love with a song or album and replay it until she couldn't listen anymore.

Wherever we lived, there was always a sweet melody, booming bass line, or video choreography to learn. My brother and I loved a few artists passionately. Our lives were all about Whitney, Mariah, Michael, and Tina. We were in elementary school when we saw *The Jacksons: An American Dream, What's Love Got to Do with It, The Bodyguard, The Preacher's Wife,* and *Waiting to Exhale.* We were probably too young to be watching those movies, but Mama was always there to answer any questions about what we didn't understand. She knew how much we loved them. Passion always won against censorship in our home.

We were most in love with Whitney's voice and Michael's feet. Mama would wear her hair long, and run into the wind, my brother and I saying she looked just like Whitney Houston in the "Run to You" video. My mama was the most beautiful woman in the world, and the only person who was comparable to her in my mind, was Whitney.

When it was just the three of us in that studio apartment, I loved watching my mother spin in our living room singing "All the Man That I Need," eyes closed, one hand over her heart, she felt something in herself unbound by that music. Someone out there "got" her when she needed it most. When she was surrounded by family but most alone.

Once my brother and I were old enough to realize we couldn't dance, we set about changing that as intensely as we'd ever done anything. We watched video after video, learning move after move. There was no DVR or On Demand. No YouTube. There were blank VHS tapes, but who could afford those? Instead we just had to wait for the videos to come on. We monitored all the music channels: MTV, VH1, BET, The Box. We'd learn them all and show Mama. She'd say, "Keep dancing, babies! Keep singing! My babies know that song!"

My mama encouraged us to sing our hearts open. There was music when we woke up, music in the car, music when we cleaned, music at family get-togethers. She would sit in the kitchen and watch us perform. She'd smile and clap for us. When my sister grew old enough to remember the steps, my brother and I would make her the star. We'd put one of my grandma's old wigs on her and make her the little Black Shirley Temple to our overly enthusiastic backup dancer roles. She would become the best dancer of us all, a natural talent who never needed our coaching.

By the time my mom got back to the car,

we'd finished singing and were on to more important discussions like what movie we were going to pick. She did a quick scan to make sure everything and everyone was still in their place before getting in, then pulled off toward the video store where the flashing lights invited us to take part in an extraordinary cinematic experience.

We took home two movies that night. The drive home was short and dark, and in no time at all, the four of us were piled onto my mother's mattress, watching *Forrest Gump*. I was captivated by the film, the classic soundtrack permanently imprinting itself in my mind. My sister fell asleep almost as soon as the movie started, but toward its ending, my mother tucked me under one of her arms, and held my brother under the other. She looked each of us in the eyes, and smiled. Her happiness filled us both, and we smiled back, comfortably snuggled against her. It felt familiar, like the time we spent together in the triplex, before I moved to Missouri, and came back different. Now, I knew that family was everything you needed to make a new start. This was our home. Nothing bad could get us here.

13

Once, my mother asked me and my brother why we didn't like Allen. She stood at the kitchen counter, smoking a cigarette and watching us while she waited, with uncharacteristic patience, for us to answer. My brother and I looked at each other, careful not to let our faces say too much before we decided whether or not it was actually safe to speak. This could be a trick. On its face, the question didn't seem to have a right answer, but we knew better. Even when there were no right answers, there could be wrong ones. And we paid for the wrong ones. I spoke first, as usual, and said simply, "He's mean."

That seemed safe enough. We all knew that, right? I'd seen him purposefully turn away from her when she tried to hug or kiss him. I'd seen him mock her in front of our family, while she laughed weakly and said, "Come on, Allen, stop . . ." I'd seen him grab my toddler sister by the arm and drag her out of my mother's room, leaving her to cry in the hallway, banging at the bedroom door, while they both giggled on the other side. Wasn't all that being mean? It had never occurred to me before that moment that my mother *didn't* think he was mean. I just assumed she liked him that way.

I thought back to the summer, when Allen, trying to be funny, ran me off the sidewalk and into the side of a brick building during a "family bike ride." The next day I woke up with a sore and swollen wrist. I showed it to my mother, and she told me to see the nurse about an aspirin when I got to school. I didn't like the taste of aspirin, so I didn't go to the nurse. The ache was a distraction throughout the day, but when it got too bad, I tried my best to zone out completely. Any pain I ignored long enough usually subsided. This pain didn't. After lunch and recess, it became clear I had a problem that wouldn't go away. My wrist continued to swell, but now I could feel my heartbeat in it, and holding my pencil was almost impossible. My teacher sent me to the nurse, whose eyes widened at the sight of my arm. She gave me a Tylenol, and sent me back to class. Right before the end of the day, she stopped by my classroom, and handed me an envelope to give to my mother.

I dutifully handed over the note after school. I hadn't gotten in trouble, so I didn't even try to read it so I could defend myself later. My mother hit the wall before she finished the first sentence. She came barreling out of her room, finger pointed directly at me.

"You went to that school and made a big stink about your arm! Now they're saying I have to take you to the doctor! Don't you know, if you make a big deal about stuff like that, they'll take you and your brother and sister away from me? IS THAT WHAT YOU WANT?"

My mother begrudgingly took me to the doctor where they told us my wrist had been fractured. When she told Allen, he laughed.

Didn't she know then?

In the kitchen, my brother piped up to add that Allen didn't like us, and seemed mad at us all of the time. He kept looking at me while he said it, and my mother followed his gaze. I wanted to tell him to stop looking at me, or she'd think I'd told him to say these things. She broke in, "Don't sit there and act like that man has never been nice to y'all or done anything for this family. He has helped me pay gas bills, car notes, electric bills, when *nobody* else was helping me. *Nobody* else is helping me."

That he was paying bills for us was news. Confusing news. I couldn't figure out why he was paying bills in a house where he didn't even spend the night. I knew I shouldn't say that, and internally admonished myself for even having the thought. If I wasn't careful, my thoughts showed up on my face before I could correct them, and I would pay for that too. I looked at my brother to see if he was confused as well, but he was looking at our mother. He looked ready to run.

By the time I turned back to face her, she'd donned a mask of fury. As my brother prepared to flee, I collapsed into myself. My mother stood from her seat at the counter, and my brother flinched. "Y'all just don't like him because he's not your daddy! BUT YOUR DADDY'S NOT HERE!" She gesticulated wildly, only stopping her rant to take short drags from her cigarette. "It's just me here . . ."

She inhaled, exhaled, then turned to my brother and me. "Do you want me to be alone forever?"

My mother insisted we were trying to keep her from being loved by anyone who wanted to love her. I wondered who my mother thought I was, or what she saw in me that told her I wanted to steal her joy. No part of me wanted to hurt my mother, not even when she hurt me. But I could see it when she looked at me, real fear, and a deep belief that I was making choices with malicious intent against her. I was ashamed by what she thought I was capable of, ashamed of whatever it was about me that made her think I wanted her to have a bad life. My shame, for her, confirmed my guilt.

When my mother told us she was pregnant, I knew it meant that Allen was never going to go away now. For a little while, that's all it meant. But my mother kept growing, and she kept bringing home these black-and-white sonograms of the baby. Even then, I thought he was cute. Still, I knew this baby would change this house, and I didn't know yet if it would be in a good or bad way. I'd been fascinated by babies since the birth of my little cousin Tyler. He was the first one that interested me. He was born two weeks before the Fourth of July, and so, he has always felt like the best part of summer to me. I remember sitting beside him, rocking his car seat during the fireworks. He was beautiful. I hoped my mother's baby would be just as beautiful. But not too beautiful. Not so beautiful his father stuck around more than usual.

About halfway through her pregnancy, I heard a commotion outside of my room, and walked into the hallway to find my grandmother standing in the doorway of our only full bathroom. *Did Mama fall?* I thought, and moved behind her to see or hear or whatever I could. Over my grandmother's shoulder, my mother sat in a bathtub full of water like a boiling meatball.

My grandmother held out the cordless phone in one hand, and fussed at my mother, "He can't just ask you that! Why can't he respect you as the mother of his child? I can't stand his ass!"

I stepped back, knowing I wasn't supposed to hear what I was hearing. However, what I'd seen had been enough. My mother's face, depleted, dead-eyed, staring into the water, while my grandmother gave her another piece of her mind. Nobody disliked Allen more than my grandmother, and it was a constant point of contention between her and my mother. I slipped away. They were always arguing, and if I heard too much, I got put in the middle.

The last time I remember seeing my mother pregnant was in her eighth month. She was doing my hair. I sat on a pillow between her legs, her belly hard against the back of my head while she parted my hair and greased my scalp. Two of my aunts laughed and chatted beside her while I was mostly ignored, as I preferred. I couldn't read while getting my hair done because I couldn't see without my glasses, but I could daydream. Something outside my bubble tugged at me, slightly raised voices. I tuned in just enough to make sure I wasn't the cause of the ruckus, only to find them talking about something that made them all mad, but didn't concern anyone in the room. Someone's man had hit her during an argument.

I heard my mother say, "Words are words, but you should be man enough not to put your hands on a woman."

This piqued my eleven-year-old interest, and I spoke before I thought not to.

"But you hit us."

My mother pulled my hair back, so that our eyes met. I was warned.

"I'm not a man," she said. "I'm a woman." Her sisters laughed, and I was embarrassed. I curled into myself, ready to drift back into my bubble. And then, I didn't.

"Well, are you *woman* enough not to hit us?"

My mother's palm cracked against the side of my head. I had been warned. I tucked my body in and put my hands behind my neck. I figured she'd yell, scream, swipe at me a few times, and be done. But . . . she didn't stop. I tried to go back into my bubble, imagined a shell around myself strong enough to take the crush of her fury against my body. The blows kept coming until they ceased in a moment, and I saw one of my aunts restraining her, while the other pulled me up and toward the front door. My mother screamed from the kitchen, "GET HER OUT OF HERE! I DON'T WANT TO SEE HER!"

On the ride to one of my aunt's houses, her husband turned to me and said, "You can't upset your mother like that. She could lose the baby." I spent the whole weekend away from my home assuming my mother didn't want me anymore, and having everyone around me give me melancholy looks as if that just might be the case. Then Allen showed up. His temperament was unusually congenial, almost conspiratorial. He told me he knew how my mother could be a lot sometimes, and the admission made me feel a little safer, like maybe I could trust him.

He asked what I thought the problem was between me and my mother. "I don't think she likes me," I said. It felt true.

He leaned back on his heels and looked

surprised. "Wow," he said. "Wow."

Early the next morning, he picked me up and took me back to my mother's house, but he didn't stay. I was relieved. He'd been kind to me in my aunt's driveway, but I was still wary of his presence, and how often it encouraged pain over peace. My mother said hello when I came through the door, then directed me to sit in a kitchen chair she'd moved into the bathroom to do my hair. I sat, half asleep, in the chair, comforted by mother's strong palms against my scalp. I closed my eyes to relax, and stopped resisting her attempts to move my head around as she constructed one ponytail after another.

"I hope you know I was crying in church yesterday," she said. "Allen told me what you said. That you feel like I don't love you. Do your really think that?" When I opened my eyes, she was looking at me in the bathroom mirror.

That wasn't what I told Allen, but I wasn't surprised he'd altered my answer. He took every opportunity to make her feel worse about herself, and I hated he'd gotten the chance to use me too. I looked down before answering, "I didn't say that. I said I didn't think you liked me."

She snorted in response, and asked without really wanting an answer, "What's the difference?"

My mother came home from the hospital after having Jorian, draped in a punch-red maternity dress covered in pink and orange blossoms, my grandmother holding one of her arms, and an aunt holding the other. My mother's face was tight with pain, fear, and exhaustion. She looked like everyone was bothering her, and I didn't want to add myself to the list, so I slipped back toward the family room, and sat on the floor. I hadn't stuck around to see the new baby who was still being detached from his seat in the car. I heard him before I saw him. A loud whining call first whistled then bellowed as it grew closer to where I sat. I was curious to see the face of the screamer, my brother, this little tether to a man I considered a nightmare.

He was red, but that was only from the crying. As he calmed himself, and slowly returned to a less enflamed shade of brown, someone laid him on the couch to change his diaper. I watched as his two feet were held in one hand, and lifted. His bottom was wiped, then powdered, then placed, gently, into a soft cloud of diaper. I was fascinated. He wrapped his small, thin fingers around my smallest finger. I fell in love.

Jorian was born with teeth. It wasn't a full set, but there were at least two little nubs. My aunts made a lot of jokes about how my mama had better not try to breastfeed that grown man baby. My mother was thirty-three years old when Jorian was born. Allen was even older. My grandmother put her fingers in the baby's mouth, felt around his gums for these unlikely teeth. When the pad of her index finger ran across them, she snorted.

"That's what happens when two old ass people go and get pregnant. They end up with an old ass baby." She shook her head at the baby dangling in the crook of her arm. He stared back at her, pushing his gums together until they bled. He was beautiful, and watching him grow was my favorite thing.

In lieu of a baby gate we couldn't afford, mama repurposed our coffee table and used it to split the living room from the kitchen. The baby was getting to be pretty mobile. No steps yet, but everyone could see, it wouldn't be long.

She'd gotten free passes to Indiana Beach from her job, confirming our annual trek to the struggling sensational amusement park, and this time Allen was going to drive us. She asked R.C. to get the baby dressed. He picked him up and attempted to step over the table. He dropped the baby, and six pairs of hands rushed to his aid. My mother saw the blood first. She held the baby's mouth open with two fingers, and saw that he'd lost a tooth. I spotted the tooth in the carpet, picked it up, cleaned it off, and put it in a small jar of sand I'd gotten from Indiana Beach the year before and kept in my room between an old Christmas ornament and my favorite book.

My mother was frantic. If Allen found out about the missing tooth, he might not take us to Indiana Beach. No one could tell him or allude to what happened.

Halfway to Indiana Beach, Allen stared hard into his rearview mirror.

"What's wrong with that boy's mouth?"

My mother said she didn't know. The rest of us stayed silent. Jorian grinned at his father in the mirror.

The car pulled over to the side of the road. And Allen turned to my mother. He announced to the car that we would turn around if nobody told him what had happened to his son. She finally did, the words coming out fast and apologetic, explain and excusing in equal measure. He called her a piss-poor parent. He sneered at her. "Maybe that's why your kids don't even think you love them." I gaped at him. He was using my feelings to hurt her, and I wanted her to hit him for the transgression against us both. I wanted her to tell him that she was a good mother, I wanted her to yell at him about how horrible some mothers can be, and break down why she was the opposite of them. I wanted her to scream and fight and be angry with him the way she got angry with me. Instead, he pulled back onto the road unscathed, and she stared straight ahead, down the length of highway, like even if she turned in her seat, she wouldn't see me sitting there behind her.

14

I was constantly prepared to fight because of the bullying introduction I'd received after moving back to Indiana so many years ago, or maybe it was the tension at home. But I was almost never interested in following through. I had a knack for deescalating those tense moments with an on the spot joke or reenactment of some comedy skit we all knew.

At least one fight broke out at school every week, and I took part in one or two of them in a given school year. One time a boy told me my mother was ugly, and I fought him so hard I ended up with a reputation. *Ashley Ford will fight boys.* I liked that. Fights were a big deal because they could get you kicked out of school, but they weren't a big deal between students. You could beat somebody's ass on Monday and be swapping notes on Tuesday. In most instances, whatever the problem had been between the two of you, the fight settled it.

We were a small underfunded school full of poor underserved kids, and even when we fought, we knew we were in it together and that we were all we had. We fought like family. We didn't choose to be here, but now that we were, we were all curious about who we would become. We wanted to be good, as all children do, but as young Black children learn sooner than others, we don't all get the chance to be seen that way.

I wasn't popular, but I was well-liked among my classmates, and I liked them too. I was weird enough to be interesting, without being so weird I made anybody uncomfortable. This was my sweet spot. It gave me room for odd interests and performative tendencies. I could be funny as long as I could stand being a little lonelier. And I could. I didn't need much.

I didn't bother to hide my strangest parts from anyone weirder than me. At that point, hiding was only done out of insecurity, or a contextual sense of propriety. It's hard to not know you're weird, when you are. The world will either tell you directly, or isolate you into understanding that something about you rubs others the wrong way. I believed you could learn to outsmart your personality, but I knew you couldn't hide from people who really saw you, and saw themselves in the part of you that tended to be just a little bit bent to the left. No matter what you wanted to hide from yourself, you couldn't hide it from the people whose particular brand of bent matched yours. The effort was moot. Weird kids always find each other.

I met Bradley during my last week of sixth grade. The first time I saw him, he was staring at me. My teacher was leading a discussion about a book I'd read three year earlier, and I'd fallen into one of my familiar daydreams. I ran the palms of my hands down the front of my jeans. I liked feeling the denim caught between layers of my skin. I was careful only to engage in the pleasure of the back and forth motion when no one was looking, or at least, no one I cared about watching me.

In my daydream, I was the teacher at the front of the classroom, arms waving with the excitement of explaining something you've known a long time, but still love to share with the others. My students were not daydreaming. Their eyes were locked onto mine, riveted by me and my ability to shoot my hard-earned knowledge like a laser straight into their brains while entertaining them at the same time. My teacher was talking about some boring book, but the class in my head was learning about *The Bluest Eye,* a book I'd recently read in three mornings in the school library. I still didn't think I fully understood, but I tried.

My fantasy faded, and my hands stilled in the middle of my thighs when I caught movement in the doorway. Well, not really in the doorway. He wasn't under the frame, where the teacher would have had no problem seeing him, but against the wall, across the hallway. And staring right at me. He was a white boy I hadn't noticed before, which was kind of hard to do in a small school that every single year had less white students, and hadn't had many to begin with. Still, I didn't know him. I hadn't ever seen his short light brown hair or soft blue eyes before. I smiled at him because he seemed weird, so it didn't matter if he thought I was weird too. He smiled back, but didn't stop staring.

"Do you have somewhere else to be, Ashley Ford?" I turned slowly toward the front, and brought my hands together, refusing to move too quickly and seem startled. Mrs. Miller stood at the front of the class, a piece of short white chalk in her hand, still pressed firmly against the board where she'd stopped writing midsentence to address my lack of engagement. I was embarrassed to be called out, and my heart punched the inside of my chest with heavy thuds. I did my best to make my breaths small and controlled. I couldn't stop the thumping, but I could wear the mask. I could show them only what I wanted them to see.

I smirked at Mrs. Miller, and leaned back in my chair. "I'm right here. Did you need something from me?"

She pushed her lips into a thin pink line, and turned back to the board. We'd almost made it to the end of the academic year, and Mrs. Miller in her smock dresses, and round wire glasses, was done battling with me. Already we'd had it out over my sneezing too loud, talking too much, reading ahead, and disputing her assertion that we must all write every paper in cursive because it would be required of us in high school and college. I didn't mind rules, but I didn't appreciate being lied to by adults, and when I saw or heard it happening, I couldn't shut up. Mrs. Miller desperately wanted me to shut up. And if I'm honest, I enjoyed making her feel that way.

When the bell rang, and we all shuffled out the door, the boy whispered in my ear, "I think you're really pretty." It shocked me down to my toes. Before that moment, a boy liking me meant he grabbed me, said crude things to me, or made me feel nervous and unsafe in some other way. Bradley told me I was beautiful and I just let the word travel from my ear to the center of my preteen heart. He hadn't grabbed or taken anything from me to make his point. He had offered me a bit of himself, the way he saw me, and I was as touched as anyone could be by the gesture. It felt like the kind of compliment that came along far too rarely, the kind you could keep without suffering for it in advance.

Still, I felt like I owed him something, so he didn't take it back. I thought about him all day, and if I got the chance to close my eyes for long enough, I could feel his breath on my skin, and hear the exact tone of the ringing bell in the background as he professed his admiration. Years of love poems, romance novels, and young-adult books that spoke directly to the budding lover in me, unfurled in my mind, reminding me just how much I'd looked forward to being wanted this way. It made sense it would take someone I'd never noticed who came out of nowhere to love me.

Bradley thought I was beautiful, but he didn't know me at all. That was probably for the best. The closer he got to me, the closer he'd get to the bad in me, and that would not do. There was no beauty in my badness, and there was no hiding my badness from anybody who got too close.

For him, I was good. When I made him laugh, his eyes sparkled, and he smiled, revealing his gap teeth, stained a faint yellow. It made me think of the Alfred E. Neuman comics in the *Mad* magazines I read five at a time at the library — if that guy lived in a trailer and was a fourteen-year-old pack-a-day smoker. I felt addicted to the way Bradley talked to me about me. It reminded me of my father's letters telling me I was the best, the greatest, the most beautiful, and the only one. I didn't believe a word, but I believed that someone else did, and as long as I could maintain that, it would be enough for me. I ached at the thought of Bradley not telling me I was beautiful anymore, and simultaneously prepared for that time to come.

After a week of stolen chats before school, and more whispers about my beauty, I thought the least I could do was give him my number. He called me immediately after I got home on the last day of school. I didn't tell my mother. I was twelve years old, plenty of girls I knew had "boyfriends," but my mother would only see one thing in any boy or man she saw me around.

"Can I tell you something?" I could hear a smile in his voice through the phone line, and I smiled too.

"Of course," I said.

"I love you," he said. I could still hear his smile, but mine fell. This was the first time we'd ever spoken on the phone, and even though I wanted to be loved ferociously and completely, it seemed like it should have taken more than this to get here.

"How do you know that?"

I heard him take a deep breath before putting his smiling voice back on to say, "I just know."

It shouldn't have worked, or maybe it absolutely should have worked on a twelve-year-old sad Black girl in Fort Wayne, Indiana. Here was a boy offering me what every other girl was becoming obsessed with: love. I wasn't sure if this was love for me, but it seemed like the kind of thing you jumped into and figured out later like all the happy couples on television.

"Okay," I said smiling again, my mind made up. "I love you too."

Christmas was approaching, and my uncle Clarence and his wife came and got me and my brother for a surprise trip to see my father. I don't know if my mother expected him to show up out of the blue, but she let us go with him. I trembled with excitement, and held my brother's hand in the back of the van. The night before the visit, my uncle used his new camcorder to record me singing "Silent Night," my favorite holiday song that year. "Wow." He watched the video of me singing, rewound it, and played it again. "You have to sing for your daddy tomorrow." I wanted to, but I couldn't imagine it happening.

Back in the van, hours away from seeing our father for the first time in years, I asked my uncle Clarence why my father was in prison. He turned off the music, and looked at his wife, who met his eyes. Then he looked at me and my brother in the back seat. "Nobody ever told y'all . . . ?" I shook my head. "Well." He shrugged. "This might not be the right visit to talk about that."

I saw my father through the small window of a heavy locked door separating me from him. He was already looking at me. He found my eyes and held onto them. In all my life, no one else has ever looked that happy to see my face. He was surprised by our visit, but not by me. He knew me. When the doors opened, I walked toward him, and he opened his arms to me. I laid my head on him and, in a roomful of convicted felons, found the only place I'd never be anxious to move on from.

My uncle Clarence said, "She wants to sing for you." And I did. I sang "Silent Night" slowly and carefully, and with all my heart. Everyone in the waiting room clapped when I finished.

My father held both my hands, and said, "Wow. How did I have you?"

That was the last I'd see him for a long time. But I thought of him every day.

15

Bradley said he loved me so much and so often, I thought it would be mean to tell him I didn't feel the same way. If all it took not to hurt him was to do a little pretending, that seemed okay. I did that all the time anyway. I wasn't great at it, but I figured it would be worth it, in the name of love. Besides, I thought, people always think I'm great at first, and then they find out I'm not. At least Bradley was just a boy who didn't even live in my neighborhood. He wasn't family. When he got tired of me, when all the good feelings about me left and he saw I offered nothing to replace it, he would leave on his own, and I would probably never see him again. I could be patient long enough for that to happen. To be sure I didn't hurt him, I could wait.

He was two years older than me, but only one grade ahead. I thought I wanted his attention, but I was grateful we had no classes together, and running into him in the halls always left me with a sick feeling in my stomach. He would want to hold my hand or scrape a dry kiss across my cheek. He went after my lips every once in a while, and sometimes I allowed them to land. That wasn't a good idea. After he'd crossed that boundary, he wanted to cross another, and another, and so on. Pretty soon he was pulling me just out of the sight line of teachers, parents, or whoever happened to be around so he could put his hand under my shirt and squeeze my growing breasts. It hurt me, and I didn't like it. I told him that, and he told me I was beautiful and he loved me. That meant he couldn't really help himself. Nothing he said felt right to me, but I didn't quite know what to say to correct him. Up until that point, one of the only things I liked about our relationship was that I had no desire to be physical with him, and therefore believed I was in no danger of shaming God or my mother by having sex before I was married. I thought not wanting him would be what kept me safe.

My cousin said having your first boyfriend is how you know you're starting to become a woman. I didn't want to become a woman. I felt like my father hadn't gotten the chance to see me as a child, and it seemed the closer I got to adulthood the less I should be seen by anyone. He was missing the best parts. Even this so-called rite of passage, he was missing it. My father would not be there to embarrass me with bad jokes in front of my friends, or look at me with disappointment when I brought home a bad grade. There would be no yelling matches, or fights over what was or wasn't appropriate clothing to wear outside of the house. No one I dated would ever have to sit through a lecture about my safety, or even the slightest hint of a threat regarding sexual activities and my young age. No one would know him, and he wouldn't get to know the best of me. The me I felt like I was losing. My father had been in prison for so long. I believed every good thing about me had come from him, and him alone. I couldn't imagine how much better I'd be if he were around. How much better we'd all be.

There was no way to tell my father about the small victories or catastrophes in my budding young adult life. He couldn't help me solve the problems I'd created for myself. In some ways, I was grateful. He didn't have to see what I felt I was becoming. He didn't have to watch in disgust as my body grew into something that could only be perverted, something I couldn't stop from happening. This wasn't the part of my life where I wanted him to meet me. I'd dreamt of that moment, and it had always been so much more beautiful, I had been so much more in that world. Out here, in this world, I felt myself being dragged down a path toward adulthood, but I wasn't done swinging on the playground. I wanted my father to know me while I might still resemble the girl he wrote about in his letters. In those letters, I was still his little girl. I still had flowers in my hands, and sunshine in my eyes.

My desire for a physical representation of my father's love led to me pursuing parental relationships with all kinds of authority figures I came into contact with. They weren't all aware of their parental status, but they were all important to me. Combined with my mother, they made up the perfect parental figures: proud of me, hard on me, and charmed by me. They were my Danny Tanners, Carl Winslows, and Aunt Beckys. Not only was I not their child, each day I got closer to not being a child at all. My body was changing, as were my thoughts, and I was terrified by them. My mind was caught somewhere between extreme longing for love and tenderness, and the fear of being mishandled, or misused.

Even as I was drawn to connect with the people around me, I feared them. Afraid of how much they might come to mean to me, and how terribly I would have to mourn when they inevitably left me behind.

At night, I'd sit in bed and say to myself, "Everyone leaves. You'll be okay. Everyone leaves. You'll be okay." I'd say it over and over until I could picture them leaving, until I could feel the tears on my cheeks. When I cried, I thought I could feel some of that inevitable pain, sparing my future self. It burned right in the center of me, and rolled my gut, but it kept my heart right where I thought it should be: inaccessible past a certain point. I did not mind getting hurt as much as I minded being surprised by the pain. I wanted to see it coming.

The adult men in my community noticed my body was changing before I did, and they did not hesitate to keep me updated. As I became a teenager, the parts of me I had largely ignored made people uncomfortable, in some cases downright angry, and they really needed me to know that it was my fault. I was walking home from middle school when a man pulled his car over and asked me for my phone number. I stared at him for a beat before saying the only thing I could think of: "I'm thirteen."

He looked as if he didn't believe me.

"Go home and tell your mama she needs to be dressing you like you're thirteen. You almost didn't get treated like somebody's child." He spit out of the open driver's window in my direction, then sped off.

I stood there, shaking, surveying my jeans and T-shirt. What about my clothes said I wasn't thirteen? What about me kept telling the rest of the world I wasn't a child? I walked home, already knowing I wouldn't tell my mother what just happened. He hadn't touched me, and I didn't want to upset her for nothing. We lived on a corner lot, and I was sometimes lulled to sleep by the sound of cars idling at the stop sign thirty feet from my bedroom window. That night each idling car set off an alarm system inside my body. I alternated between finding a spot on the wall to stare at and drift, and curling up into myself trying to cry as quietly as possible.

A week later, my mother stopped me as I climbed into the car. "You need to change your shirt." It was my favorite shirt — denim with puffy sleeves and a mostly Lycra bodice. It was tighter than it had been three months ago, but still pretty, and still my favorite. I dragged my feet on the return to the house. The rest of the family was already in the car, my grandmother in the passenger seat shaking her head. She turned to my mother.

"When did she get so . . . big?"

My mother sunk into the driver's seat, watching me walk away. "I don't know. But it's only a matter of time until I have to choke somebody for looking at her."

I let the screen door slam, walking quickly toward my room. I grabbed a long white T-shirt from my top drawer, something I usually slept in. I changed out of my jeans and into baggy overalls. Nothing to see here. Nothing to touch.

I'd started wearing the overalls to keep Bradley out too. He was going to change schools when his parents saved enough to move out of their trailer and into a house. It meant his dad would have to be transferred by his job, and the whole family had to move to a smaller city just north of Fort Wayne. Whether or not they would go was up in the air for a few weeks before they decided. His mother was reluctant to leave. She would miss her family. In the end, none of them could vote against moving into a house and out of the trailer park. When it was still a question, before they'd settled on it, when he called me every night crying and telling me we didn't have to break up, I

161

prayed that when they moved away, he would forget my name at the county line.

Long-distance was too hard, and we were too young. That's how I'd explain it to him, I thought. That's how I'd make him understand. And I did. That night on the phone, my fingers curling in my grandmother's comforter, I told Bradley, "If I give you all of me, and you give me nothing back, then what do I have? Less than nothing. Less of me, and none on you."

"You don't have nothing," he said. "You have me. And one day, I'm going to give you everything. When we're married, you'll have all of me, and anything else you want in the world. I would die to give you everything." It sounded like love in the movies.

"No," I told him. "I don't want to do this anymore."

I told Bradley I'd see him one last time. He asked me to come to the meeting spot easiest for me, where we could be alone. No one ever went in or out of the white storage shed in my mother's backyard, and though it was dark, cold, and dirty, it was private. We could talk there, and no one would be any wiser. This time I knew I could convince him that our relationship was over. We were kids, and he was mean, and I just wanted to be good. Couldn't he let me go so I could be good? When I walked through the door, and shut it gingerly behind me, the light from outside moved quickly across his face. I could see he had been crying, and the tears had begun to frost in the cold.

I hugged him because I didn't want him to hurt, and he clung to me, his heaviness pushing my back into the discarded washer or dryer just behind me. I let him cry into my shoulder, and tell me how sorry he was, and how sometimes he blacked out, and how he just didn't want me to hate him. I told him I didn't hate him. When he said, "I love you" I started to pull away. "Don't do that." He gritted his teeth, and tightened his grip around my waist.

"Bradley," I said, falling back into a soothing tone for a shot at a safe exit. It scared me how easy it was to hear that sugar-sweet dead voice come out of me. It wasn't me. It was whatever he needed me to be, and I didn't want to be her. I could be good. I could have straight-A report cards and special field trips, but it wouldn't happen if I was stuck talking to him like this for however long that may be, and to a thirteen-year-old, almost any time at all feels like forever.

"Please," I said, this time speaking like myself. "I don't want to hurt you. I just want to say goodbye. Can't we just say goodbye and be friends?"

My eyes were just starting to adjust to the dark, when he dug his nails into my sides, a boy made of fury, and growled, "No." I didn't scream. I didn't know who would come or what they would think was happening when they got here. It hit me that I had made all the wrong choices when I walked into this shed. The weight of his body shifted from my front, as he leaned back and pulled me up onto the top of a rusted metal washer/dryer, held both my wrists in one of his hands, and used the other to fumble with the zipper of my jeans. Every time I attempted to yank my arms or legs away from him, they hit the sides of the machine, causing a deep and hollow BON-NNNGGGG to scare me into stillness.

"I love you," he said, his face dripping with tears and snot and cold sweat. "Please," he said. "Please."

I didn't know what he was asking me for, but I didn't want to give what he was taking. My thoughts scattered and separated, silently running down our list of options and coming up short for a way out. I thought I saw something move in the corner and prayed it was the rat-cat-coon my grandma told us burrowed beneath this dump. Anything that might bring him to his senses, provide the single moment of interruption when he realized what he was about to do and decided not to. But it wasn't an animal, mythical or otherwise. It was Jerry. Bradley's friend. Watching us and hiding. Bradley wasn't going to change his mind. He was doing exactly what he'd come here to do. He lowered my pants and underwear with one hand, and the cold metal of the washer collided with my skin like a million needles. I was out of time to think. Nothing and no one was coming to save me, and since I could not save myself, I went away. I closed my eyes and let someone else take my place. I floated off into the frozen day, toward the weak sunlight breaking through a sparse set of clouds.

It had never been this hard to get back into my body. On the shed floor, my back to an icy metal appliance, and my front curled in and around itself, I looked like a slug who was trying to sleep or die. I was there, and I was desperately trying not to be, and then I was gone. There was something in me that felt too good — too innocent — for what was happening to this body that kept getting me into trouble. When I realized what was happening, what he meant to do to me, what he'd already begun to do to me, inside I screamed. My mind split. It stayed silent to stay safe on the outside. But in my body, a word traveled from the tips of my toes, to the top of my head, and it said to that small sweet part of me, the only loved part of me, "Run."

I couldn't imagine who would have wanted to stay there. A long time after both boys slipped out of the door, hopped over a fence, and snuck through my neighbor's backyard, I tried slipping back into places like an arm, or a foot, or an ear. Each time, a pain, sharp and cold, bit at me, warning me to stay back. It felt like I'd spent hours with my mind hovering above my own body, terrified to fully enter and find it cold, or worse, empty. I didn't know how long I'd been there, and I could only be sure of at least one thing having happened, but I still felt like I was missing something. I began to cry, and my brain began to wake to the alternating pain and numbness in my hands. Panicked I might have to explain the pain to someone if I couldn't control it, I shook my hands until my whole body was shaking, and then I couldn't stop the shaking. I shivered and shook until I was able to drag my sore body from the shed in an upright position. I hoped I wouldn't draw attention to myself. Halfway back to the house, I turned and looked at the shed, thinking I should go back. *I left something,* I thought. *I left something important in there, and it's too cold to go back for it.*

My body, and whoever lived in it now, walked back into my house. I met her there. She tried to tell me what had happened, but I wouldn't let her inside.

16

I stopped wanting to go home. I wanted to be somewhere that was safe, where I wasn't alone. No one questioned why I wanted to spend so much time in and around school. Sure, I'd been in trouble a few times for behavioral issues, but I was still known as a smart and curious kid. Maybe even, in the right light, at the right time, charming.

School was safe. I was stronger there. I stood up for myself there. I didn't want to go home. I still cried all night, and slept too little. I stopped going into the backyard. Since my mother wasn't home from work by the time school ended, it didn't take long to realize if I just didn't get on the bus, I still had a few hours before I needed to walk home and be there by the time she arrived. It was risky. She could always come home early, find me missing, and be boiling by the time I unlocked the door. Then there was Bradley. He could always be waiting, knowing there was a better chance she would be gone, and that I would be unprotected. I'd take my chances with my mother's rage.

After the last bell of the day, I would walk to my locker, collect my coat, book bag, and a few folders, then slip into the nearest bathroom where I would wait until I could no longer hear voices in the hallway. About ten minutes after the silence, I'd hear the long groan of several school buses pulling out of the parking lot, one by one. I'd count them, until the last one faded. Only then would I push open the bathroom door, careful not to make noise, or be noticed should anyone be closer than my ears assumed. When the coast was clear, I'd step into the now-silent expanse of my educational institution. It all seemed bigger when I was there alone, and I felt bigger too. If I ran into a teacher, I'd explain that I was staying after for some activity or another, and they believed me. Sometimes, I would visit the parts of the building where a few kids really were participating in practice or a meeting for a sport, team, or other student group. I could slip in and chat a bit with the few kids, make them laugh, and be moving on before I was caught. Whatever I'd lost in the shed, it was good to know it wasn't this ability. Being invisible was still my super-power.

I tried not to think of what had happened to me. Most of the day, I could succeed in that mission. Then, a shock of ice-cold air on the wrong side of my face. The rattle of plastic meal trays against the hard metal counter during breakfast and lunch. Feeling too sad, or feeling surrounded, and I would be back on the roof of the shed, looking down at myself, pathetic and mumbling nonsense. I hated that place. I hated every-thing in my view, including the ball of rot-ten nothing called my body curled into itself on the floor. Why didn't she get up? Why didn't she go away? She never should have been there at all. Staring down at myself, I admonished her, blamed her, and only spoke enough to say, "Stop bothering me. Stop bringing me back here. We don't belong to each other anymore. You made the choice to go in there. Now you can stay there."

My after-school wandering kept me from having to go back. I was the best of me somewhere in between the drab school walls. When I left them, I was nothing. And nobody cared what happened to nothing. And everything happened to girls who were nothing.

It took three weeks for me to figure out who the other stragglers were and perfect my rounds. First, I'd visit with my choir teacher, Ms. Wagner, for as long as it took her to pack her things and head out to her forest-green Subaru. She was my favorite, one of those I'd initially found prickly, but she didn't like to dawdle after hours, and I did not blame her.

After that, I'd visit the student groups, and make my way down to Mr. Unway's classroom. Mr. Unway was my social studies teacher. He was one of the few people who seemed to genuinely enjoy my questions, so I asked a lot of them. It made sense to me to keep that same rhythm after school was done for the day. I would just stand in the doorway and ask him questions. I tried to make them interesting to him, noting ideas that had come up during class, or sharing some slightly deeper research I'd done into relevant subjects. He would chat with me, and answer my questions, and then I'd move on. Whatever we spoke about was usually pretty boring, and I felt no need to hang around. It wasn't Mr. Unway, who was a very nice man. It was that I needed to move.

The point was to wander. Stopping in and speaking to teachers was just a good way to hide. If a teacher, staff member, or any other adult should come down a hallway and see me, they would be suspicious of my presence. I wasn't supposed to be there. But if I was standing with or talking to another teacher, the suspicious party, eager to mind their own business, would simply accept that I was under someone's care. I was there, a reason to be concerned, and then, with a quick wave of rational thought, I was gone from their mind again.

Almost two months into making my rounds, I ran into Mr. Martin. He was my computer teacher, and I didn't like his class at all. In fact, I regularly slept through it. My body's continued refusal to sleep through the night meant I couldn't stay awake when I was bored. I couldn't control it. Where I had once been able to daydream myself away in moments of weak concentration, I now found nothing but a sweet and impolite slumber.

SMACK! A teacher's hand would come down against my desk, just beside my cheek. The louder the smack meant the more offended they were. Some teachers would call out to me until I woke. More than a few classmates gave me a swift kick or a quick elbow when they caught me fading. Sometimes, they just let me sleep. Mr. Martin never let me sleep. Mr. Martin watched me until the moment my head began to droop, then he would simply say, "Ashley Ford." And continue his lesson. When one of the boys in my class thought to make fun of me for it, I mocked him for his rat tail until the rest of the class laughed, and he cried.

Mr. Martin was locking up his classroom, and I couldn't avoid him. He was in the same hallway as the last unlocked exit, and I was supposed to meet my brother at the library before heading home. Before he could ask me where I'd come from, or what I was still doing there, I started to ask him questions. He answered my questions right up until we were standing in front of the truck of his car. He opened the trunk and its only contents were an entire case of Mountain Dew and a huge stack of our local newspaper, the *Journal Gazette.* I asked why he had so many papers. He heaved his bag on top of them, and said, "I deliver them in the morning." I was confused. Why did my teacher have a paper route?

"With your kid?" I asked.

"What?"

"You take your kid on *their* paper route, right?"

Mr. Martin smiled at me, but his eyes looked tired. He reached into the trunk, grabbed a Mountain Dew and a newspaper, then handed me both. Mountain Dew wasn't my favorite, but I loved reading the newspaper when I could get my hands on one. I started to walk away with my new things, when he stopped me, "What do you say?" I thanked him. He smiled a little. "See you tomorrow, Ashley Ford."

When my mother came home, I was sitting at our kitchen table, the paper laid out before me. I stacked the sections by least interesting to most interesting, starting with the sports section and ending with the comics to maximize my chances of reading the whole thing. I did read it all. Any day I could, I visited Mr. Martin and got a Mountain Dew and a newspaper. I said thank you, and he said he would see me tomorrow. I liked him a lot more, but that couldn't stop me from falling asleep in his class, which I continued to do. Interrupting a lesson to say my name had stopped working, and letting me sleep was out of the question, so one day, Mr. Martin kept me after class.

The bell rang and I moved toward the door. "Ashley Ford, I need you to stay. I'll write a pass for your next teacher." My classmates looked at me with big eyes, and I swear Rat Tail giggled. Being held after class usually meant you were about to be in real trouble. The kind of trouble the teacher didn't even want to bring up in front of the other students. Everyone here knew why I was being asked to stay after, and most of them were probably wondering why it had taken so long. For a moment, I thought I should say something, explain what seemed to be happening in my body, and how the old ways weren't working for me anymore. I wanted to defend myself. Then I was back on the roof of the shed. Just where I didn't want to be.

"Sit there." Mr. Martin pointed at the student's desk closest to his. I sat. He was going through papers on his desk, putting them into folders, and putting those folders into drawers. He didn't speak, and I was glad because at that point, I could not have responded. I heard the shuffling of notes and assignments beside me, and I followed the sound back into this moment, and away from the shed. I wanted to take a deep breath, but didn't want to look like I needed one. My brain screamed, but I maintained my composure until I no longer had the desire to take heaving breaths. He was already talking by then, and I'd missed a bit. I listened closely until I could trust myself to know what was going on, as if I didn't know what was going on. It was the sleeping. It was distracting. It was disrespectful. I had to do something about it. *Yeah,* I thought. *I know.*

"Is there a . . . reason?" He asked the question like he wasn't even sure he wanted me to answer, which was fine by me. He tried again. "Is something . . . happening to you? Something that keeps you from sleeping?"

I began to laugh. "Yeah, being afraid of the dark is happening to me." It wasn't a lie, but it might at least sound like a joke. Mr. Martin did not laugh with me. He sat back in his chair and looked at me, until I felt forced to look away. I wanted to be seen, but I didn't want to be watched. He turned around in his seat, fumbled through his bag, and handed me a cassette tape.

"Just play it while you sleep at first," he said. "Then try playing it with just your closet light on. Then try playing it with no lights on. It helped my daughter when she was little. It might help you too." I looked down and read the label: *Return to Pooh Corner.* I put the tape in my pocket, and stood to go. I'd gotten to the door before I threw a "Thank you" over my shoulder.

A few days later I was asked to stay after class again, this time by the teacher who liked my questions, Mr. Unway. "Ashley, do you think your behavior toward me has been at all inappropriate?"

Inappropriate. I hated that word. It always meant that the breasts I hadn't asked for were moving too freely, my most comfortable shorts were too small around my ever-growing thighs, or my body was betraying me in some other way. I said, "No."

"Do you think that hanging out in my classroom before or after class in small clothes is something a nice girl would do?"

I wrapped my arms around myself. My clothes weren't small. They were a little tight. My body kept growing, but only in certain places. I did my best to cover up, to hide it, to keep looking like someone's little girl, but I was visibly losing the battle, and had been for some time. It wasn't just me. We were all changing. I enjoyed peeking at the other girls in the locker room while we undressed. It was hard to ignore their maturing bodies, or stop comparing them to my own, but I didn't want to make them feel like I felt most of the time. I didn't want to make them feel watched. Did they hate this too? Did we all hate this together, but cry about it separately?

Mr. Unway picked up on how uncomfortable I'd gotten and asked if I'd come speak to the principal about this with him. I followed him out of the classroom, and into the hallway because it seemed right. He walked five steps ahead of me, and as we rounded the corner toward the principal's office, I spun around and walked in the opposite direction. By the time he called out for me, I was already running toward home and my tape player.

When Mr. Martin asked why I didn't come around anymore, I made something up about babysitting my siblings. He had been kind to me. He'd helped me. But I was not his daughter, and my clothes were too tight, and I didn't want him to die. Any kindness that existed between us was bound to be tainted by how I looked and how that made any interaction rife with the potential for wrongdoing. Who I was inside, who I wanted to be, didn't match the intentions of my body. The outside of me didn't present a little girl to be loved innocently. My body was a barrier.

I took solace in the tape that helped me get over my fear of the dark. Kenny Loggins sang to me the way I wanted my fathers to speak to me — with wisdom and love and the belief that I could still be good. I gave up on the men I knew in real life, but I couldn't give up on the man whose voice found me in the dark.

That was the beauty of Kenny's music. I never have to grow away from this safe space. The voice on my tape, a celluloid dream or memory track, didn't know me in real life. He would never have to watch me grow up. He would never have to consider me appropriate. He only had to sing and remind me I was still here, in this body. Every part of me was still here.

At the end of the school year, Mr. Martin caught me in the hallway on my way to the bus, and handed me a laminated bound volume of the ramblings I'd written in his classroom. "You wrote a whole book," he said. "Don't forget you did that."

17

In all my hallway wandering, it was never my intention to settle in any one place, so I didn't. I didn't want anyone to get too close — and I didn't want Bradley to come looking for me. I walked down the halls, occasionally listening as an announcement came over the intercom. They were always announcing awards or accomplishments. My name was never called, but one name was always on or at the top of the list. Brett Tubbs. I hated that name. Day after day I rolled my eyes at the mention of this Brett Tubbs, who I did not know and hoped I would never be so cursed as to gaze upon. It was only a matter of time though in our small school.

I wanted to hate him so bad the first time I met him — the first time he made me laugh. I'd walked into the classroom where the newspaper club would be meeting, and saw his name on the board, listed as one of the students expected to join. I rolled my eyes, and found a seat with my back to the wall, the entire class in front of me. I sat there, fuming at the idea of him, of potentially having to work with him, and then he walked in. He smiled at me as I glared at him, and said, "This will be fun. The teacher's kind of a dumbass." Yes, I despised the idea of a goody-two-shoes boy, so good at doing whatever adults told him to do, too dumb to know none of it mattered. But that wasn't Brett.

Soon, my hatred turned into a deep and urgent pining. Brett exuded a sense of control over himself, and over his life, and I was drawn to his steadiness. His love for music helped too. By the middle of the semester I was working on the school newspaper, playing intermural soccer, and had fallen in love with color guard, and most of it was because of him. I didn't even know myself, but I liked myself. Maybe I did hate the idea of him. But the reality of him made me feel like I had never been less invisible, like I was finally safe.

He asked me to join color guard, and then marching band, and because he had gone from nemesis to necessary in my mind, I made it happen. Well, we made it happen. In band — at least in our band — nobody was supposed to have to do it alone. I didn't have to rely on my mother for rides to practice because Brett would pick me up, without complaint. Mr. Caffee said if we were five minutes early, in our places, ready to go, then we were on time. If we arrived at start time, we were late. Brett was never the kind to be late, so I was never late. It felt good to show up morning after morning and know I'd already done the first thing right. It felt good to know that Brett would always show, pulling into my driveway at the same time, every morning. The consistency of it, knowing he would be there when he was supposed to be, felt as warm as all the best summer days. The good Fourth of Julys. Marching band took up most of my time, and I liked it that way. It kept me from thinking about home or anywhere else.

Being away from home meant being away from my siblings, and I hoped less of me in the house would even out to be for their own good. Even if it wasn't, it was what I needed. To be separate. My presence brought tension, and I told myself being away was the only way we were going to make it out.

Even when I was home, I tried to be gone in some other way. Lost in music, lost in a book, and often lost in another phone conversation with Brett. That's who I was talking to when I heard the front door unlock, and the heavy smack of Allen's boots against my mother's linoleum entryway.

I sighed into the phone. "Allen is here." We continued our conversation, content to ignore his arrival, when my bedroom door swung open. He stood in the yellow-lit doorway, rocking back and forth on his heels, his hands clasped behind his back.

"Where's your mama?"

Barely looking up, I told him where she was, running late from work or running an errand, or whatever was true. I didn't try to be pleasant. I'm sure I rolled my eyes, or seemed impatient. He knew I didn't like him, and I felt no need to hide.

He released his hands and held up a plastic bottle. Allen thought my little brother should be done with bottles by now. I didn't know if he was right or not, but I agreed with my grandmother when she said, "If he wants him to stop having a bottle at night, then he can come actually stay with his baby at night."

Even before Jorian was born, it was rare for Allen to spend the whole night in the house with us. Even if he stayed late, in the bedroom, or out in the living room halfway holding court for a few adults who'd come to visit, I always heard his car peel away at some point in the night. I listened to my Kenny Loggins tape on a low volume in bed each night, but sleep still came later for me than everyone else in the house. If I knew he was staying, I turned it up a little louder. He was always saying things I didn't want to hear.

He held the bottle in front of my face and said, "Y'all know I don't want this shit in the house." I looked from side to side, not worried exactly. One of the biggest arguments my mother and I ever got into was right after Allen had spanked my sister for annoying him. I'd yelled that he wasn't her father and wasn't allowed to touch her. I told him if he ever touched her again, I'd call the police. My mother yelled at me. She told me to shut up. She told me he paid bills that my sister's father didn't pay. Allen smirked, threw his hands up, and walked out of the front door. My mother kept yelling. She told me I had to go out and apologize. I spoke to him through his car window. "If you ever hit me, or any child that doesn't belong to you, ever again, I will call the police. And I won't ever stop calling the police." That felt like a good warning to me, so I didn't expect he'd ever forget our terms of engagement.

He stepped back into the hallway and slammed my door.

I heard a cracking sound in the kitchen and walked out to find him stomping on the plastic bottle. He wasn't really succeeding at breaking it, and looked ridiculous in the act. Brett was still on the phone, which I spoke into as I watched Allen. "Okay. He's losing his mind." I rolled my eyes and turned back toward my bedroom. I walked into my room, shutting the door behind me, but it stopped short and bounced back. I turned just in time to see Allen coming toward me, hand outstretched. He grabbed the phone from my hand, then brought it back down across the side of my face.

"Get the fuck out of my room!" I exploded. He'd hit me. This monstrosity of a man had crossed my line. Not again. My mind rattled with fantasies of how I would get him back. Brett was no longer on the line, but I was sure he'd heard what happened. Allen left my room, and I sat down on my bed. After a couple minutes, I found myself packing my book bag full of underwear and special things. I thought of every place I'd ever felt safe, and found the list sparse. Maybe any place was safer than here. I knew that wasn't true, but sometimes, I wondered. I put on my coat, opened my bedroom window, and climbed out.

The headlights on my mother's car were just dimming as I fell onto the bush outside my window. She opened the car door, stepped out onto the driveway, and stood there staring at me, confused and angry. Another set of headlights came around the corner and pulled up behind her. Brett was in the passenger seat and his father was behind the wheel. My mom looked at them, then back at me, and finally at Allen standing in the doorway.

"What's going on?" she asked. Neither of us answered. I walked right past her, and toward Brett's window.

Her voice rose, and she asked again, looking back and forth between where I stood and where Allen stood, "WHAT IS GOING ON?" I ignored her, looking at Brett instead.

He looked right back at me. "Are you okay?" he asked. I nodded and tried to smile, but the attempt made me look even more pitiful. Brett leaned toward me, unblinking, lowered his voice and said, "You can come with us right now."

The fear that my mother may have heard him forced my best imitation of a real smile to my face, as I shook my head and said,

"No, it's fine! I'm okay. I'll see you tomorrow." He looked skeptical, and so did his father, but there was nothing they could do or say to make this better for me. We all knew that was true.

I didn't look at my mother until they'd rounded the corner, out of sight. When I finally did, she was already in a state. "What the hell were they doing coming to *my* house? For what?! I could expect something like that from Brett's mom, but his Dad is *Black.* He at least should know better than to come to *my* house to check on *my* child!"

"He came to check on me because *your* boyfriend hit me with a phone." I looked at Allen. *I told you,* I thought. *I told you I would tell, and I did.* He looked back at me. My mom looked back and forth between us. Then she settled on me, her face hardened.

"Bullshit," she snarled. She didn't believe me, and I hated myself for being hurt by it when I should have known better.

I felt like I was choking on my own life, drowning in it. My home didn't feel safe. My mother was in love with a cruel man. Bradley was still calling my friends, and their parents, asking them to send me messages. They didn't know what had happened, but they could sense things weren't right — maybe even that I needed help. In more than one uncomfortable conversation, I asked a friend's parent not to pass on the messages, and maybe, if they could, to block his number. One night he called the mother of one of my girlfriends. He told her he had a gun to his head, and asked her to give him one reason why he shouldn't pull the trigger. She hung up.

The next week, Bradley and a friend showed up during a late-night band practice. The band was rehearsing a show on the blacktop next to the tennis court as the sun set behind the rolling formations. My friend, the girl whose mother had taken that awful call, spotted him before I did. My bandmates closed in around me, and Brett quickly led and devised a plan for distracting Bradley and his friend. He walked a small group over to Bradley and tried to engage him with conversation, while my bandmate, Ryan, hustled me into a car and drove away. Just as I strapped myself into the passenger seat, I heard a knock on the window. Bradley's face was red, swollen, and barely restrained. He held up a photo of me, my school portrait, grabbed both ends of the picture and began to tear it into smaller and smaller pieces. Ryan peeled out of the parking lot, and when I asked him to take me back, he kept on driving me home.

I rested my forehead against the cold window, barely registering the passing houses, streetlights, or which road we took. It had been the right thing to run away from Bradley, I knew that, and yet I continued to cry, believing I had hurt him, rejected him, and that the fury I saw in his face was my doing, and mine alone. I felt like my father would understand me, if I could just tell him what was happening inside me. I wanted to tell him everything, to confess the bad parts of myself and have someone say, "I still love you. That will never change." I looked for my father, for his unending love, in the faces of every adult around me. I knew he would know how to protect me. He might even know how to help me protect myself.

18

In my father's absence, my grandmother did her best to stand in. She'd never heard of tact, but she was still a harbor in the stormiest days of my childhood. She was not warm and endlessly loving as I imagined my father to be. She was real, and as real people often are, she was complicated. She had a critical streak and it cut deep. And if my mother didn't like feeling distant from me, my grandmother found it untenable. She insisted on being the solitary place I sought guidance outside of God, but she did not always feel safe to me, and I hated that about myself. I didn't want it to be that way. I felt her need for us to be close in the way she still gripped my hand when we crossed the street, and I blamed myself for my inability to ignore my feelings when they came between us.

In the throes of my deepest anxiety, it's her voice I hear warning me of Other People and what they might say. At first, I didn't know who Other People were, nor did I understand how concerned I should be about their perception of my actions good, bad, or otherwise. But I spent so much time with my grandmother, and she spent so much time talking about Other People, I eventually had some idea about the bad things they might say about me. They might say my clothes are too big, or small, or maybe even that they look old. If I'm hypervigilant about my personal hygiene, they might tell others about the time I used to stink. They might not be there for me. They might not love me.

My grandmother didn't see this as gossiping or being critical. She thought she was being helpful. Her fearful desire not to be "talked about" expressed itself as a constant monitoring of Other People's behaviors and presentations of themselves, and she offered swift judgment whether the behavior or presentation was good or bad. Most were bad. This frustrated her to no end. Why weren't people more careful? What kind of woman left the house without wearing lipstick? How could anyone let themselves get that fat? Who raised them? Who let them become this way? Didn't they know Other People would talk about them?

My grandmother would sneer at and side-eye anyone on the street, but especially women she thought underdressed, mismatched, or sloppy. The stakes, she had impressed upon me, were too high for women to fall asleep at the wheel of our own potential. She believed that for women, beauty was as much a requirement as an opportunity. What were you going to do with yourself if you weren't going to be pretty? I don't think I ever saw her take joy in applying makeup or getting dressed, but when someone else noticed the time and effort she'd put into her appearance, she'd give them a small closed-mouth smile, and nod her thank you. Her eyes would sparkle. If Other People were going to talk about her, she was going to choose what they talked about and how.

My grandmother couldn't understand how every woman and girl she met wasn't exactly as concerned and deliberate in her choices. When she caught sight of these careless women in the wild, her lips would tighten. It was unladylike, I had learned, to speak ill of others at a volume in which they might actually hear you. My grandmother, ever the lady, would lean closer to my ear so as not to offend the offender. Her musky perfume sat heavy in the back of my nose, and if I opened my mouth and breathed it in at the same time, it tasted like the warmest version of my oldest memories. She spoke in a low voice, her slight Southern accent curling the ends of her vowels.

"Now you wouldn't ever see me out here looking any kind of way. Thank god I raised all y'all better than that."

As a child, I would nod or stay silent. My opinion was neither desired nor required. When my grandmother spoke that way about Other People, she was reminding herself of something she believed more than she was discussing the merits of her life choices with me. The never-ending barrage of criticisms she hurled in every direction was often funny, and I assume, at some point, compulsive. She didn't lie. She really believed she was keeping herself safe, and her family safe by holding us all to the same impossible standard. Somewhere along her lifeline my grandmother had gotten the idea that Other People's opinions could kill. With her criticisms and corrections she hoped to build a wall of perfection around herself and those she loved. As a family, we might face trial and tribulation, and we may even let our hair down, but not for Other People to use as ammunition against us or our family's name. The sharpness of her words were meant to hook into our soft outsides, toughen us, shield us, and become our armor against the prying eyes of a stranger's judgment.

Being my grandmother's favorite meant being watched. Sometimes I wanted her to take me away, but after a while, she made you feel bad about yourself. She could be loving and protective and funnier than anyone else I've ever met, but her criticism was incessant. I may have spent more time with her than most of her other grandchildren, but I was not spared, though I did enjoy the very real fringe benefits of her rare and enduring bouts of generosity. We shopped together almost as much as we watched old movies together, not that we had much money to shop with. My memories of various shopping trips are mismatched and often strung together, the markers of time being the size I was wearing that year, and how she reacted to that bit of news. I remember dressing rooms, attendants, accessories, and credit card offers. Every time a salesperson asked my grandmother if she was interested in their credit card she would say firmly, "No, not today. Thank you." They may have been trained to bring it up more than once, but after she spoke, no one ever did.

This particular afternoon she was supposed to take me to the Glenbrook mall. I'd been sulking because my mother and I had gotten into an argument about Allen earlier in the day. "You just don't like him!" She always said this to me when I complained about something he'd said or done, and I couldn't defend myself because she wasn't wrong. So, I would say just that.

"I don't like him! I don't! I have no reason to like him!" Then she would tell me about respecting adults, about the bills he paid, about how no one else was helping her, and I knew I'd lost. To be fair, I always lost. Still, it seemed important to keep fighting when it felt like the right thing to do.

Our argument ended with me fighting back angry tears and my mother pacing the house and intermittently opening my door to tell me another reason why I was wrong. I knew I'd made a big mistake. If my mother got angry enough, or if she worried I'd talk about any of this with my grandmother, she wouldn't let me leave to go shopping. There wasn't anything I wanted more than to get out of the house, and I might have just incinerated my only guaranteed chance to do that all weekend.

My grandmother walked into the house with the weight of our battle still hanging in the air. "Ashley, let's go," she said. I ducked into the living room where my mother was folding clothes and told her Grandma was ready to take me to the mall. She looked up at me with a hard stare.

"Don't run your mouth. Everything you feel ain't for everybody to know." I nodded, and left the room.

After we locked the door behind us and walked down to the bus stop, my grandmother turned to me. "You and your mama got into it?" I shrugged. She looked down the street like she might see the bus, then back to me. "You not gonna tell me what it was about?"

I didn't like the way this felt. No, I hated it. I hated it when my grandmother asked me about my mother because she wasn't going to help me, not really. She would listen, and sometimes she would even agree with me, and that used to feel like enough, but that feeling was fading. What would be enough? I didn't want to talk to her about my argument with my mother because it wouldn't help me, and she would use it as a way to criticize her daughter, and I didn't want to hear that. For maybe the first time, I told her I didn't want to talk about my pain. For this, she was offended.

We shopped our usual department stores,

JCPenney, Sears, and Macy's, mostly in silence or with the occasional "Do you like this?" followed by a simple head nod or shake. Getting new clothes was not a given when we came to the mall, but my grandmother made sure I always got to grab a little fast food at the very least. When we finished browsing, we headed to the food court. We got in line at Panda Express. It was the always longest line, but I loved the opportunity to people watch. I scanned the various restaurants and their patrons. I tried to imagine their lives backward from the moment they stepped into that line. I wondered what they'd had to say or do to find themselves there and how many of those steps they wished they could take back. I was always wondering about somebody else's regrets.

"You should be nicer to your mother." My grandmother spoke to me, but looked straight ahead in line. We were the same height now, and I turned to her, confused. Then I was mad. She didn't even know the whole story. She was taking my mother's side of an argument she hadn't seen, heard, or even been told about. I closed my eyes and felt a tug in the air above me like I was being lifted. I began to move my feet in a rhythm, rolling from heel to toe, standing in place. To anyone else, a bored teen shifting feet from side to side. To me, a soothing motion I'd learned from marching band, a way to stay inside myself when my big feelings tried to push me out.

When I felt safely tethered again, I spoke, trying to keep my voice measured. "Yes, we need to be nicer in the house, but I disagree that it needs to come from me." I knew my grandmother was baiting me, offended I hadn't opened up earlier, but I tried to defend myself without offering any details about what had gone down between me and my mother. Maybe she just wanted to hear me talk about what was on my mind, but I denied her. And even though I felt I was ultimately right, I didn't want to see her upset by my caginess.

Lost in my thoughts, I didn't notice my grandmother's face ripple with frustration. "You need to be nicer to your mother because you don't even know why your daddy is in prison."

Her hard tone should have been a warning sign, that now was not the time to talk about whatever she was suddenly willing to confess, but my curiosity blinded me. I wasn't sure yet that I wanted to know, but I hadn't been this close to an answer since that car ride with Uncle Clarence. He'd already been so good to us by bringing us to visit our father, it would have felt ungrateful to push him on the subject. But I didn't bring it up this time, my grandmother did. I wanted to know more than I was afraid to know. My chances of it coming up again anytime soon were slim.

"Why is he in prison?" I took the shot I had, and waited for her to answer.

"He raped two women."

My grandmother blurted it out like it was just another nasty piece of gossip. My feet stilled. I masked my face, showed no emotion. I didn't want my grandmother to decide I couldn't handle what I'd heard, which I wasn't sure I could. In my family, showing too much emotion got you labeled. I'd been told I was too sensitive for a long time, and I didn't want to prove anybody right. Crying in a mall food court wouldn't help. There was always the chance that if I looked like I might fall apart, she would stop talking. I didn't want her to stop talking. I didn't speak.

After a few moments of silence, she added, "Don't tell your brother."

I rubbed my gurgling stomach. Aside from the pain I felt in my middle, I'd gone numb from head to toe. My body continued to move, but once again, with the sense it had left some irretrievable part of myself behind us. Gone and here. Between here and gone. Always alone. I told my grandmother I didn't want anything to eat anymore. That was not a lie.

This was an old game we played, my grandmother and I. She told me secrets, and I pretended to have never heard them. The game usually started differently. Usually, she would begin by telling me something, then stopping before adding details, peering at me from the side of her eyes, and saying, "Nah, I ain't gonna say nothing else 'cause you'll tell it. You always tell things!" And I would protest, "No, I don't tell things!" Then she would mention a time I *did* repeat something I shouldn't have, most likely an example from a time before I was six years old, and I would defend myself as not a six-year-old, and then, finally, she would finish. The reveal was rarely worth the work, but it felt so good to have someone want to tell me secrets and trust me with them. This one I regretted knowing. This one I tried to forget, not because I should, but because I really really wanted to.

I tried to not make a memory of that day. I'd been too curious — I'd spoken and let the demon in.

I kept myself from crying for the rest of

the trip while my grandmother pretended not to watch my face. I was good at this. Control your breath, quiet your heart, die on the inside, only let them see life. Normal life. I stayed steady until five minutes after walking through the front door of my mother's house. I picked up the cordless phone, and called Brett. I asked if I could come over for a moment. He said I could. I set down the phone, turned back toward the front door, and I left.

I walked to Brett's parents' house on autopilot. I crossed roads without looking both ways. Brett was waiting for me. I saw his head through the little windows at the top of the door. I put on a bright smile, and waved to his mother who was smoking a cigarette and curling her hair at the kitchen table. We walked the three stairs down into the den, and sat on a love seat. Then I told him everything I could, which wasn't much, before dissolving. He scooped me up, and cradled me in his lap. He rocked me back and forth, and whispered into my hair, "I'm so sorry, Ashley. I'm so sorry."

I shivered and shook against his chest, and he held me. He didn't let me go.

That night I dreamed I'd lost my glasses in the shallow woods next to my mother's house. I dreamed I ran through the night, aware that I was being chased, but unable to name or describe my assailant. Without my glasses, I couldn't find my way through the trees in the dark, and I panicked more and more with every step. Eventually, I would convince myself to sit wherever I stood, and wait for the sunrise, or for whatever was coming to find me in the dark.

19

Brett and I were best friends, and after hating him, then two years of pining for him, I finally worked up the nerve to ask him if he liked me. He responded, "I do. But there's more to it than that." *What kind of cryptic ass answer was that?* I'd thought. When he couldn't explain what he meant, he asked me to be his girlfriend instead. Good enough for me. I knew I loved him when I walked into the band room and watched him playing the saxophone, his fingers moving deftly over the keys.

We started dating a few months after I told him about my father. Sometimes, he asked me how I was feeling about my grandmother's confession. I don't remember what I said, but I must have lied. I tried not to feel anything about what I'd learned, and I did a very good job of that for a long time. Sometimes, I couldn't help it. In the stillness of the nights that kept on coming at the end of every day, no matter how pleasant or productive the day had been, I wondered if something was wrong with me for ever loving my father in the first place. It made sense why everyone who knew the truth couldn't look me in the eyes when I asked. They didn't want me to feel ashamed, but they already felt ashamed for me. I saw it on their faces, pointed in my direction.

My father's crimes repulsed me, and I felt for some reason that I should have known better. I convinced myself something about his letters, his drawings, or the tone of his voice should have revealed to me what he'd done, and I hadn't noticed because I hadn't wanted to. It made sense to me. Every once in a while, my mother and I would find ourselves in the living room at the same time, watching some Lifetime original movie. Rape was in the central plotline of 75 percent of them. A few times, I caught myself wishing, out of everything it might be, that my father was not a rapist. It was my biggest fear before it was my reality, and the thought that he might have . . . I didn't think. I wished. *You should have known then,* I thought, *that something was wrong with anybody who loved you that much.*

All my life, my father represented love to me. Deep, enduring, irrevocable love. So many times I thought all the problems of my life could be solved if I'd just had him there to hold me and tell me who I am, and how much he loved that person. I never imagined pain coming from my father, or the mistakes he might have made as a present parent. My naivete shamed me, and I accepted that shame as my own. In the dark, at night, the saddest part of me assumed my father's crimes were the source of the crime committed upon me. This was the only way I knew to make the connection between what my father had done to the women he raped, and what had happened to me in the shed. I relied on Brett to distract me from both of them.

Brett loved me. He was right though, there was more to it than that. In the aftermath of the shed, the books I found assured me of something I knew in my mind, but couldn't feel in my body: I hadn't wanted what happened to me to happen to me. This was important because in the movies I watched with my mother, the women who had been raped stopped wanting to have sex. I hadn't. I thought about having sex with Brett all the time, and I worried that meant something was wrong with me. I felt like the wrong kind of victim.

As much as my mother, teachers, cousins,

grandmother, and classmates had already spoken to me about the mechanics and morals of sex, no one ever mentioned that rape isn't sex. What Bradley did to me, what his friend watched being done to me from the corner of my mother's shed, wasn't in any way the same as what I wanted Brett to do with me. All of those books with white girls on their covers in the teen section of the Hessen Cassel Branch of the Allen County Library taught me the difference. There was no one in the whole world who made me feel safer than Brett. If I was going to find out if the books were right, he would be the best person for me to learn that with.

I lay in Brett's bed, naked from the waist down, waiting for him to raid his sister's room for a condom, and replayed how I'd found myself there. I'd always thought it would be important to me to have candles, soft music, or at the very least, shaved armpits when I finally chose to have sex, but in that moment, none of it seemed necessary. I was sixteen, and happily swept up in a hormonal undertow. Brett was kind, and he was gentle. He would not make fun of me for my armpits. He never made crude comments about women, and he never pressured me into sexual situations I didn't want to be in. I trusted him to handle me with care.

And I had something to prove.

When he found the condom, and got under the covers with me, the warmth of his bare skin against mine spread to every part of my body. My muscles relaxed when he kissed me, slowly, and asked me if I was okay. I nodded, encouraging him to continue. The hands of a musician move over anything they love like an instrument. Brett was so controlled when and where he applied pressure to my body. His touch was deliberate, and gentle, and by the time our bodies joined, I was more than ready to welcome him. The minutes passed in a blur, and with love and patience, I received one of the greatest gifts of my life: the deep knowledge that I had had sex, with my own intent and will, and it had been like nothing I had ever experienced before. Nothing.

20

Too many parts of my life seemed unpredictable, much too dependent on the moods and inclinations of others. To wrangle my days and weeks into something consistent seemed out of my reach. I was hanging on, surviving by slipping in and out of the lives of those around me, tagging along, getting rides, hanging out, and being around without ever really sticking around. There was no schedule to survival. I pulled myself together to push for a B average, sometimes less, but really only so I didn't embarrass Brett who was on track to become valedictorian. Band was the most consistent thing in my life, but even that only motivated me so much. School felt like practice for white collar prison, and I couldn't really pretend to care as much as it would take to make everybody happy.

I continued to read everything I could get my hands on, especially if it hadn't been assigned in class. My teachers were frustrated, but for the most part, they liked me and thought I was smart enough to engage. A few of them talked to me about going to college, but it was a touchy subject. I loved the idea of going to college, but the reality was, I didn't think we'd be able to afford it, and when I thought of the reason why, I had to swallow hard and try not to burst into tears.

Back in middle school, every day for a week, I asked my mother to submit my paperwork for 21st Century Scholars, a state program that promised to pay the college tuition of low-income students who maintained at least a C average through graduation, and then attended an in-state school. A few of my teachers, Mr. Martin included, had pulled me aside multiple times to make sure I was getting the forms signed and turned in. He asked if I wanted him to call my mother, to nudge her. I made it very clear that would not help me. If my mom thought I was talking about her not doing something, especially with my teachers, I wouldn't hear the end of it. The time she'd spend being mad would be more time than I wanted to deal with it.

The last time I asked my mother about the papers she told me if I asked for them again, she would throw them away. She never mentioned them after that, and I made myself stop thinking about it too. On the day of the deadline for submission, I hid from the teachers who were most likely to ask me what happened. I didn't want to tell them my mother forgot. I didn't want them judging and talking about either of us for not being able to get it together. Even when it was the truth, she would never forgive me if I told these strangers she'd messed this up. For months afterward, I walked past those teachers in the hallway reluctant to meet their eyes, terrified I would find them looking for answers, and that I would be persuaded to provide them. College seemed like the kind of experience you had to plan, and I already knew I was no good at making or having plans, or keeping plans, and I had no one to make or keep them for me. If I was going to go to college I was on my own, and I had no faith in my ability to be enough to get it done. In some ways, I'd already given up.

There always seemed to be some more urgent need right in front of me at school or at home. My mother's house could be as peaceful as it could be chaotic, it just depended on whatever happened that day. Not one of us was immune from coming home carrying the ire of some earlier confrontation with a classmate, coworker, or other irritant. On the worst days, we carried on for hours yelling, hitting, hiding, crying, talking, and hiding again. We rushed through rapid cycles of joyful bonding, and soul-stunning violence, but it was never on the calendar, and I never knew when it was coming. If anybody in our house had a plan, nobody let me know.

Those bad days seemed to come less often once I started spending more time away from home, but I had to have good reasons to be gone. In theory, my mother believed in trusting me until I gave her a reason not to. In practice, like most other mothers I knew, she needed to know where I was going to be, who was going to be there, who their parents were, and how long I'd be gone. I still had more freedom than most of the other girls I knew, and began to feel like something might be shifting between my mother and me. Even though I didn't have dazzling grades, I made up for it in my mind by being involved in every student group where I might have even the slightest interest, as long as the schedule didn't compete with marching band. I was spending more and more time in practices, rehearsals, and club meetings, but on the rare occasion I was home before she went to work her night shift as a correctional officer, my mother might stop me in the hallway and say, "You know I'm proud of you, right?" And while the delivery would be a little aggressive, I would smile and say, "Yeah, Mama. I know." Then she would remind me of a chore I needed to do, or bring up something else that had nothing to do with how she really felt about me. I knew she missed me. I thought that was the only reason we were getting along.

A friend told me she was going to visit her boyfriend in Muncie on the Ball State University campus, and asked if maybe I wanted to come along. Her boyfriend had also been in band my first summer, but he'd already graduated by the time I got to high school. Though she was a year behind him, they had kept dating, and I admired their long-distance commitment. My freedom may have extended beyond the boundaries of my peers, but there was no way my mother was going to let her teenage daughter drive down to a college campus for an evening of whatever the hell. I was about to say never mind, when I heard Allen laugh somewhere on the other side of my bedroom door. The sound grated against my inner ear like an abrasive pestle. "I'll ask my mom if I can come. I'll call you back."

I didn't want to be home. Allen was often present, working on somebody's car he kept in my mother's garage, and I didn't think I could handle spending any more time around him. I called my mother and told her I had to perform in a neighboring county with the band. I may have even named Bluffton, though it was too early in the season for that parade. I knew she wouldn't know either way. She usually didn't ask too many questions about band trips because Mr. Caffee was the only white man she trusted for miles, and I had never lied about them before. I said my friend would pick me up and bring me back home.

My friends were usually utterly charmed by my mother — she was her most magnetic around them, or anyone else on the outside really. But this friend had met my mother when she was wearing her correctional officer uniform, and she'd been afraid of her ever since. I knew my mom liked it. "It's better," my mother said, "that she worries about what I will do to her if something happens to you." If my mother found out about the lie, I knew she would come down on me. *Too far down the road,* I thought. *The consequences of your actions here are too far down the road.*

The ride into campus, just as the sun set on the bell tower, felt enchanted like the opening scene of a teen rom-com. It occurred to me no one would be able to tell I was a high school student. I was excited to pretend, if only to myself, to be someone more than who I was, like a student with direction and a notebook full of plans. Someone starting over. We met my friend's boyfriend in his dorm room, and he already looked older to me. He drove us all to a local pizza place nestled in a little collection of campus-adjacent restaurants, bars, cafes, and shops appropriately referred to as the Village. After pizza, we went back to his dorm to hang out for a bit but hit the road back to Fort Wayne before too long. Our stay wasn't more than a few hours, but to me the whole place was out of a storybook, quaint and magnificent. On the way home, my friend told me she'd applied to Ball State and had gotten in. I was happy for her, that she'd gotten what she wanted. I told her that was the first college campus I'd ever really been on.

When I got back, my mother never suspected a thing. I used my key to unlock the garage door, tiptoed through the living room, and crept into the kitchen to quietly release the cordless phone from its cradle.

Undetected, I slipped back into my bedroom, and called Brett. When I confessed to him what I'd done, I told him being on campus made me think I might try to go to college.

He released a breath on the other end of the line. "Of course you're going to college, Ashley."

That was news to me. My mother had always said I could be whatever I wanted, but she felt no need to push me. If I said I was bad at math, she agreed, and I continued to do my best, now with a confirmed belief that I was bad at math. I wasn't sure how hard I was supposed to try to develop skills I saw as hopeless. My mother wanted me to have my own dreams, so she feared dreaming too big on my behalf. "My mother was always in my business," she would say. "I'm not doing that to my kids."

Nobody else had set a college expectation for me, I assume for the same reasons I hadn't set one for myself. I wasn't a little kid anymore, and aside from Brett and my friends, I didn't even get birthday presents anymore. Who was supposed to have money for me to go to college?

"You'll find that out after you apply and get accepted." Brett's tone sounded like I should know better, but he didn't want to hurt my feelings by just saying that. "If you get in, then you can apply for financial aid. Jesus, Ashley, you have to try. Why wouldn't you?"

Later that week I went to the public library, and started researching options for an academic future I wanted, but hadn't dared to dream of. I was tired of being disappointed, and it seemed that disappointment started with wanting things. I tried not to want. There was a new program at our school where a few students were chosen to spend half the day, twice a week, taking a course at the local community college. The other three days of the week we would meet with tutors who would help with our coursework. We'd all been selected based on our testing scores, and since it was a small school, I knew everyone else who had been chosen. The class would be free for us, but the credits would count toward a degree should we go on to pursue one.

I signed up for the college class to prove a point. My current English teacher pulled me out into the hallway on the first day of class and told me she knew what kind of kid I was — that I hung out with smart kids to get away with rudeness. She told me exactly how I was going to behave if I wanted to stick around. I told her if she didn't take her finger out of my face, I was going to keep it. The principal told me I was too smart to be acting out. I told him he hires teachers who don't like children.

What started in middle school as normal teenage expressions of antiauthoritarianism, or as many of those as a Black girl has access to, exploded into full on contempt for most of my teachers and administrators by the time I was a junior in high school. There were a few teachers who I respected, and felt truly cared either for me and the student population they served. Everyone else, I had reason to believe, was only here to assert power in unnecessarily cruel ways. I counted that English teacher among the latter. I confronted her, and my principal, with tall and hollow confidence. I knew I had almost no power in this interaction. I knew my mother wouldn't have my back in this situation, but my anger didn't care.

The only time my mother took my side was when a teacher tried to tell me a book was too advanced or too old for me, but that hadn't happened since elementary school. Now, my mother called me sneaky. "You like to try people," she would say to me, peeping at me from the corners of her eyes, her head turned slightly away. "You just like to mess with people until they don't have any choice but to do something crazy." I wanted to defend myself, but then I thought of everyone around me who had lost their minds a little, and I decided not to lie. No, my mother would be no help here. I thought of one of my classmates, who often found herself called out by teachers. If they riled her up too much, she'd start to scream, "Call my daddy! I want to talk to my daddy!" And even though we were all seventeen years old, sometimes someone called him. He always came to the school to be on her side. I thought that was ridiculous. And I wished I had it for myself.

For the rest of the day, I sat in in-school suspension daydreaming about myself in a different life, a better one, with better teachers, books, and my dad. Not my dad who was sitting in a prison somewhere for his crimes, but the one who still existed in the place I floated off to when I needed peace. He was the one I kept hold of, the one I was still trying to get to call me his favorite girl. It occurred to me, I could take that version of him with me wherever I went. Maybe I didn't have to be afraid to leave, to pursue something more. If he only existed in my head, he could find me anywhere.

When the time came, I applied to one community college, Ball State University, and one dream school. I found my mother's tax documents in the nightstand next to her bed, in the same drawer where I sometimes found old letters from my dad I didn't remember, or that weren't meant for me in the first place. She'd told me they were there when I told her I needed them to fill out something called the FAFSA. That's how I found out my mother was raising four kids with no financial assistance on less than forty thousand dollars a year. The guidance counselor who was supposed to help me finish the forms kept shaking his head, and saying, "This is going to be hard on your mother." I didn't know what he was talking about. Everything was already hard on everybody.

21

My Ball State University acceptance letter arrived in a thick cardinal-red envelope. I took it into my bedroom, closed the door behind me, and opened it alone. When I saw the word "Congratulations!" I knew. Thump thump thump, my blood rang in my ears and drowned out the world. Because I was by myself, I allowed a wide grin to spread out across my face. I held the letter to my chest, and squealed instead of screaming. Even if it didn't work out, even if I never got to step on campus as a student, I'd been accepted to college. I had been accepted.

I told Brett first. "I knew it," he said. I could hear him smiling. I wanted to wait to tell my mother until I could figure out how to ask her to help with the $125 housing deposit to secure my room in the dormitories where freshmen were required to live for at least their first year. I'd been working at the mall part-time for almost three years, but the money seemed to leak from my bank account no matter how many times and ways I tried to save. I had a job, but felt deeply afraid to drive. My grandmother hadn't had a driver's license for as long as I'd been alive, and yet somehow, she continued to be the worst backseat driver in the Midwest. "Just let your boyfriend drive you," she'd tell me. "Men are just better at that kind of thing."

But after years of shuffling me from here to there, Brett remembered he wasn't actually my parent, and refused to continue to be my chauffeur. My mother, not wanting to have to drive me around herself, gave me her Pontiac Bonneville and bought a used car that was new to her. I didn't have to pay for the car, but I was responsible for the insurance, and that seemed more than fair, definitely more than I'd ever expected. My mother was relieved to have me paying for my own gas, outings, band fees, doctor's appointments, and most of my own food. It felt good to me to pay my own way when I could, like I was finally offering my mother the relief she'd earned, but I knew I would need help with this housing deposit, and I knew asking her would be its own minefield. If she could help me, she would do so happily. That was the best and least likely scenario. If she couldn't help, she wouldn't say so, but she would eventually get angry with me for asking. Sometimes she would tell me she could help, but when I followed up she would claim I was harassing her, and now, because of my nagging, she didn't want to do it at all. Asking for help could go wrong in so many ways in my house, but this was college. I'd been accepted, and despite all I'd taught myself about wanting less, and needing less, I couldn't pretend I didn't want to chase this dream. I couldn't pretend I didn't want to see what might be possible for me. It was worth the risk.

My mother was in the living room. I walked in holding the letter in both hands. It required every bit of my ability to focus to maintain a normal gait, keep from fidgeting, and stabilize my voice. I walked toward her, and stopped just to the right of her.

"Mom?"

She stopped folding clothes, and looked at me, her expression more cautious than curious, as usual.

"What?" she asked.

I handed her the letter first, but before she could open the envelope, I said, "I got accepted to Ball State."

My mother leaped from the couch, and

screamed, "YES!" She pumped her arms up and down, her face stunned and eyes wide. It wasn't surprising that she would be happy for me, but this was something else. She spun. I would have spun with her if I could have stopped myself from watching her revel in the good news. *My* good news. She pulled me into an embrace so quickly, I felt bad for how I stiffened in response. She held me close, kissed my cheek, and I allowed my face to melt into her shoulder. I felt smothered in the intermingled smell of coffee, cigarettes, and cherry-almond scented Jergens. I felt ashamed of my need to stay there, and my inability to simply be grateful for the moment.

My mother didn't let me go. She whispered in my ear, "I knew it. I knew you could do it." When I told her about the deposit, to my surprise, she smiled and even laughed a little. "We'll figure it out. Don't you worry." I worried anyway. But before the deadline came, she handed me a check for the full amount. I didn't even have to follow up.

She went all out for my graduation party. She did so much I worried it would make her grouchy, but she remained in good spirits the whole day. We had a pool party in her sister's backyard, and even though all my friends came ready to party, I couldn't wear a bathing suit in front of all those people. My mother spent hundreds of dollars on the food, and as I bit into my uncle's ribs smothered in his super-secret barbeque sauce, I remembered why the smoky meat had become synonymous with celebration in my mind. I finished my first plate in a hurry, then rushed back for seconds before people started making plates to take home. Right before I walked into the kitchen, someone took me by the elbow and pulled me into the hallway.

"Ash," my grandpa whispered. He looked left to right and past my shoulders, then smiled like he'd already gotten away with something. There was no one around, but I whispered back.

"What's up?"

He held out his hand, palm up. In the center was a small plastic bag of what I assumed was weed. Until that moment, I hadn't seen it up close, but that wasn't because I wasn't interested. Nobody ever offered it to me, and even if they had, my mother told me she'd done it once and it made her see demons in the faces of her friends.

I told my grandpa I didn't smoke, and he looked disappointed before saying full volume, "Well shit, that's what I got you for graduation." He walked back into the kitchen and started prematurely making a plate to go, which meant he'd probably leave without saying goodbye. Usually people waited until closer to the end of an event to prepare a plate, but my grandpa always seemed to think there wouldn't be enough left for him unless he came and took his before everyone else. I watched him piling food on the Styrofoam, and wondered when it would be enough.

Just then Brett came around the corner, and asked me to take a walk with him.

"You want me to leave my party?"

He looked uncomfortable. "Just come to my car." We walked across the cul-de-sac my aunt and uncle lived on to Brett's car parked at an angle, the passenger-side mirror mere inches from taking out the neighbor's mailbox. Brett opened his door, and riffled around inside for a moment before emerging with . . . nothing. No, it was still in his hand. A box.

A box.

I considered that Brett may be about to propose, but nothing about it made sense. Blood pulsed through my ears, drowning out the world, and revealing to me a clear moment of unfiltered knowing of what I wanted. For so long Brett had been my anchor of expectation, and in my mind, my only way out of my mother's house. We'd talked about getting married before, but well into the future. He was my best friend, and I loved him, but he was no longer the only thing I had going for me. I had gotten into college. I didn't need to belong to him or anybody else to be on my way somewhere I'd never been before.

I begged myself, *If he asks, be strong enough to say no.*

He laughed at the look on my face, watching me spiral, maybe even pleased by the obvious severity of my response. He took my hand. "I'm not proposing." He opened the box. Inside was a ring. I didn't even let myself take it in before I started to pull my hand away, but Brett held onto me.

"It's not a marry-me ring," he said. "It's an I'm-proud-of-you ring."

He took it out and presented it to me, a white gold band, with a sapphire in the center, my favorite gemstone, and two almost microscopic diamonds flanking its sides. The panic left my body, and I took it in fully. It was beautiful. I loved it. He put it on my right-hand ring finger, and it fit. When we walked back into the house, the kitchen was full of people loading up on more macaroni and cheese, cornbread, and barbecue. My father's sister asked where we'd been, and I showed her my ring in response. My mother said it was beautiful, but she made me promise we weren't engaged. I promised.

My grandpa hugged me, then handed me fifty dollars. "I sold that shit," he whispered.

Right before graduation, one of my favorite teachers, Ms. R, had gotten engaged. She was going to be moving to Chicago to marry a man who loved music as much as she did. She and I had bonded my freshman year over *Romeo and Juliet* and fashion magazines. It felt right that if I was ending my time at our high school, then she would be too. I visited her at home after my party. She was packing up all of her records, vintage furniture, and other everyday trappings. She had bags of things she wanted to give me, and I was happy to take them all. After I'd loaded two Heftys full of clothes, shoes, and handbags into my trunk, I showed her my ring. Ms. R looked at my ring for a long time. She held out her right hand and asked me if I remembered the ring she wore there. I did. I'd noticed it years earlier. She told me she'd bought it as a reminder that she could take care of herself. I repeated the memory to her, and she

227

smiled, pleased. She took the ring off, and put it in my palm, closing my fingers over it. She held my hand like that for a long while.

"Brett is very nice, and that is a beautiful ring. But you have your own diamond. You don't need one from anybody else."

22

The day I left for Ball State my mother melted down. By the time I returned home from saying my farewells to Brett, with mutual promises to make the long-distance thing work, she was whipped into a frenzy about something my grandmother had said to or about Allen. I was going by the bits and pieces of conversation I'd picked up on the other side of the phone call she was having with one of my aunts.

I assumed, at some point, she would get off the phone and help me load the car with my things. She didn't. When the car was loaded, I thought she'd hang up while I hugged my brothers goodbye. My sister and I had gone to hug when my mother told her to get into the car too.

"Why am I going?" My sister looked confused. I just wanted to get on the road. My mother glared at her until she got into the car, and I followed. My mother handed one of my brothers the phone, and got in the driver's seat. We pulled out of the driveway, down the street, and onto a main road. When we stopped for gas, someone waved at my mother, and she flashed them a smile as big and bright as all outside.

During the ride to campus, my mother mostly fussed to herself about whatever she'd been talking about on the phone. I stared out the window, and counted the mile markers until I lost count, and I was gone again. My mother's voice faded into the background of my thoughts, and I pictured my new life on the other side of this car ride. Despite all my reading, my imaginings of college came from television and film, where parents cried when they dropped their kids off. They took photos or videos, and they said things they'd been meaning to say, or things they said every day but were suddenly desperate for their child to remember. Silly thoughts and dreams. I hated myself for wanting them to be real, and for believing they ever could have been. I hoped college would be some place I learned my lessons the first time.

It wasn't a long drive, and soon we pulled up to my dorm, entering the scramble of campus newbies, with creepily cheerful RAs chatting up parents. As others were hauling large suitcases down hallways and up stairs, I easily filled one rolling cart with all of my belonging and moved them up to my new room with the help of my sister. My mother scowled behind us the entire time. We pushed the cart through the door, and since my roommate had already set up her side of the room, my side was clearly designated. It didn't take long to unload everything from the rolling cart, and as soon as we did, an RA popped out of another room and asked to borrow it to help the next student. My sister wheeled it over to her, and I turned to my mother. I asked if maybe she and my sister wanted to stay and eat a meal before they left. She avoided my gaze and shook her head.

"I don't want to wait around. I don't like to drive in the dark."

My sister hugged me goodbye, then my mother wrapped one arm around me and kissed my cheek. "Love you," she said.

"Love you too, Mama." I watched her disappear down the hall, then walked back into my dorm room, alone. I did not feel afraid though. I felt free.

My love for my family was in direct conflict with my need to be gone, out, and away. My oldest brother and I, for many years, were best friends. Moving away made it hard to get him on the phone. He always preferred to drop in and speak in person. But I was not there. When I occasionally came home, I hugged and kissed them all, until they'd wriggle away from me, "Ash, stop. Seriously. Oh my God." Every text, tweet, or Facebook message I sent them was filled with exclamation points and smiley faces. My wish, and my primary motivation, was that my adventures would inspire their own. I swept into family gatherings during the holidays, a walking banner: Family, you can do this too. You can do anything I can do. But each time I left campus to come home, I spent ten minutes in the mirror reciting the same phrase like my therapist had taught me: I like myself the way I am. I like myself the way I am. I like myself the way I am. I like myself the way I am. Then, I would promise myself not to forget.

"This is the first conversation I've ever had with a Black person. So like . . . thanks? It was really nice!" I stared at the girl standing across from me. What was I supposed to say in response? "You're welcome" felt wrong. She was blond and freckled, and we'd been talking for over an hour in the study room at the end of the hall. I hadn't been a college student for long before it occurred to me that white people could grow up in a place where they never had to interact with Black people. I forced a smile, not knowing what else to do, as she waltzed out of the room, unaware, even proud of herself for taking the giant leap of directly addressing a Negro. Up until college, the school system I attended was always over 80 percent Black. That wasn't the case here. Here, I was one of only three young Black women on my dormitory floor, and that made our floor stacked.

My roommate and I were the only students on our hall who didn't own their own personal computers. It was easy enough to make do with the computer labs, and though it was something I noticed, it didn't seem like a reason to complain. Some of the others kids were getting biweekly visits from their parents, whereas I couldn't imagine anyone being able to afford that much gas. It was nice to have a break from family. For the first time, I felt grateful not to have parents or guardians who insisted on constantly checking in on me. Walking through the Village in Muncie, I would see someone sitting with their parents on the patio of a restaurant. Sometimes I would feel the familiar pangs of longing, but more often it was sympathy. It was hard for me to imagine that the child might be having a nice time with their parents even if they were good at faking it. I thought, *I am freer than you, and that is worth all the things I don't have.*

I was alone in a college town, managing and caring for myself with limited guidance. I did not find ease, but I did find temporary moments of peace. I had more direct control of my comings and goings than I'd ever had before. I could plainly see where I was already lagging behind others when it came to material wealth, and how the impact of my decisions would be tempered by that fact, but for the first time in my entire life, I didn't feel watched. My mistakes, however big or small, to the people around me were just . . . mistakes. I was never accused of plotting against anyone's well-being or attempting to ruin their day. For weeks at a time, I didn't hear anyone scream in anger, and if I did, it was never directed at me, so I felt I had nothing to fear. On campus, cloaked in the protection of emerging adulthood, I did not feel the need to court a new kind of chaos, and so chaos had to work to find me.

College became, as it has for so many others, a refuge as much as a resource. I woke for my eight a.m. course, an introduction to the fashion major, three times a week, never showed up late, and sat in the front row. I joined a community-service-focused organization called Student Voluntary Services, and used the work-study I'd been awarded in my financial-aid package to join Ameri-Corps part-time. I considered joining the band for about half a second, but I knew I wouldn't sign up. It wasn't *my* band, with *my* bandmates, and I didn't want to have that experience with anybody else. Then, after meeting with a professor in my apparel design program and being dissuaded from continuing down that path, I considered changing my major to psychology. "My mom would kill me if I changed my major," one of my classmates offered when I told her my plan. It hadn't occurred to me to mention it to my mother. When I did, she said, "Oh, well. As long as it's what you want to do." I didn't really know what I wanted to do, but I was intoxicated with the freedom to decide for myself, when so many of my more fortunate classmates didn't have that option. My freedom to choose, un-watched, became precious to me, and I felt like I might float right out of my shoes.

My roommate and I grew close, bonding over our being broke, and determined. My dorm room started to feel like my whole world, the new home base of my real life. My dining card was a marvel. Being able to swipe for food whenever I got hungry, no matter how much actual money I had access to, felt like I'd made it to the other side of hard times. What had once been scarce now felt plentiful, but the old feelings always found a way back. While browsing in one of the dining halls, I noticed my favorite flavor of bottled tea in a section of the refrigerated beverages. The fridge was usually full, but there were only three bottles of the tea I liked left. I bought them all at once. When I came back the next day, there were only three again, so I bought those too. By the end of the week, our mini-fridge was full, and I was keeping bottles of tea lined up under my twin bed, just in case I went back for them, expecting them to be there, and discovered them all gone.

I tried not to think about what might be happening back in my mother's home. I tried to call only when I had good news. I didn't want anyone to worry about me, even though usually nobody did. I learned the details of any family drama weeks or even months after the drama occurred. Most of my family was so used to everyone living around the corner, used to random but regular impromptu visits to each other's living rooms for a long chat. They stopped telling me things in real time because they didn't think to reach out. It wasn't intentional, I just wasn't there to run into. Except for my grandmother, of course, who called more often than anyone else, just to say, "Don't do anything stupid, and I love you."

Brett started classes at the community college where we had taken courses in high school. With my encouragement, he joined the theater program. The way he talked about performance made me miss our times when we'd perform together. We spoke on the phone every day, even as we were pulled into our own distinct groups of friends. I still felt a kind of desperate hunger for him, but I could also feel the threads that bound us being cut, one by one — by the days passing and the empty space on the phone line before we said good night.

When I asked him why he felt so far from me, even on the weekends when he visited me, or took me back to Fort Wayne, he looked into my eyes and asked, "Why do you need something to be wrong?"

And I wondered why I did.

23

I went home when my great-grandpa Morris died. I didn't know how to feel. When my grandmother and I lived in Missouri, he hadn't been kind to me as a rule, but he had worried when my grandmother thought my fever was too high. That was the day I saw him hovering in the bedroom door, as I laid on my side, arms and leg splayed out, drenched in sweat, telling my grandmother Jesus had come to him in a bubble and said I was going to be okay. When I caught his eyes that day, he looked away from me, and whispered to my grandmother. The fever made me bold, and I asked what he'd said. She wouldn't tell me.

When he died, he left everything to her. He'd been living in a retirement community for a while, refusing to sell his land to encroaching developers. My grandmother had always told me she would eventually leave the farm to me, but when she called to ask if I had any interest in it, I couldn't really remember what it looked like. I remembered how it felt, and how it made me feel, but the terrain itself had vanished from my memory. It didn't make sense to go back anyway. I was done with that dream, and was looking for a new one now. I told her to sell it, and she did.

With part of the earnings from the land sale, my grandmother moved out of my mother's house and bought her own. It was a lovely three bedroom, one-and-a-half-bathroom ranch just a four-minute drive away from where she lived with us. She couldn't wait to show it to me, and I couldn't wait to see it. The first thing she showed me was a small room with twin beds.

"This is the guest room," she said. "Or you know, your room, when you're here." She tossed the last part behind her as she walked back toward the living room. I smiled. I never was surprised when she made room for me.

After my grand tour of the house, I went back to my mother's. As soon as I walked through the door she started yelling at me about my bags in the family room. There was nowhere else for them to go, but apparently, I hadn't left them in the right place.

Before I'd even fully moved out, when I was working at a Boy Scout camp outside the city the summer before college, my mother moved boxes of my belongings into the garage to make more room for my siblings, and my grandmother, who was still living there at the time.

Usually, when she got like this, I got quiet and slipped away, but it wasn't working. I couldn't ignore her, my brain wouldn't drown her out, and I felt stuck. No one yelled at me, or even raised their voice to me at college, and I was out of practice dealing with the way it made me feel. She hadn't hit me in years, but when she yelled and screamed and raged, the fear of it crept over me like ice, and I hardened into defensive mode. A few weeks of not having to take anybody's shit, and I got really bad at taking it, especially as it dawned on me that she couldn't make me stay there. For the first time, as my mother attempted to draft me into this familiar dance, I could just leave.

I asked her to stop yelling.

As expected, that made her yell more. "Who the fuck do you think you are?" She paced back and forth in the kitchen, eyes fixed on me, perched on the couch. "You don't come back here and tell ME what

YOU want ME to do!"

I started to laugh, and she stopped pacing, but kept scowling. "It's fine!" I threw up my hands. "I don't have to stay here! Grandma has a room for me. I'll be over there."

My mother trailed behind me as I grabbed my bags and headed for the door, "Yeah, you just stay your ass over there! Better for you to be over there than starting shit over here!"

I got into my car and drove away from my mother's house, and the last thought of it as my home.

24

Talking had always been the smoothest part of our relationship, so I knew when Brett was hiding something. Our regular phone conversations had become stilted, and I could feel the warmth in his voice slipping away. I'd ignored what I knew to be true — even in high school.

Brett tried to come out to me twice before he actually said the words, "I'm gay." We'd both talked about the fact that we were attracted to people who shared our respective representations of gender, and many of those who did not, but we always made it a point to note that ultimately, in the mess of all that desire, we wanted to be with each other first and most. We would never give each other up, and more importantly, he would never give up on me. That's why it took so long for him to say what he needed to say. He loved me, and he wanted to want me. He didn't want to let me go.

We had been in a relationship for six years, and were best friends for longer. He was my safest place, and he knew that was the case, had seen it for himself. We didn't know, back then, there are about a million ways to love and be loved by another person. We thought what we had, the way we had it, was the only way it could be. We were stuck.

He called me first. When I answered, his sobbing choked the phone line, and I spent an intolerable amount of time saying, "What? WHAT?" into the receiver. When he caught his breath, steadied his voice, and finally said the words, I wept on my end of the call. I told him he had to come see me, in person. He had to say it to my face. I had no idea what life would look like without him, and I tried to picture it while I waited for him to arrive. He'd been my focal point, and often, the guiding force for every decision I'd made over six years. I hadn't put "me" before "we" since I was fourteen years old, not wanting to go back to being the only person in the world who really knew who I was. There was no one I trusted to take care of me more than Brett.

I knew who I was without him. I knew being apart would hurt, but it would not kill me. I had no idea what I should do with myself, or who I should ask for directions to wherever I was supposed to end up next. Was I supposed to know?

Brett was the first man to hold me with desperation. Like if he didn't hold onto every part of me all at once, he might find himself in a million pieces on the floor. Our love affair had been passionate in its way, but that's not the portion that made me feel wild with grief at the thought of losing him. It was the safety, and the acceptance of my shame. That's why it was so hard to let him go. Because of the way he held and rocked me when I told him I'd found out why my father was in prison. Because I knew no one else would ever know what I looked like curled up in his lap, soaking his T-shirt with my tears, trying to fold myself into nothing. No one else would ever see the way he desperately clung to my legs the night he came to my dorm room, and repeated that he was gay, and I tried to leave the room. Or the way he fucked me twenty minutes later and slept all night with one arm thrown across my waist to anchor me beside him. Not one person aside from the two of us would know it was the last time we were intimate with each other this way.

We made it two more months after that night. Chained to one another by time, promises, and the overwhelming fear that if we couldn't have each other this specific way, then we could not have each other at all. After everything, he still let go first. I held on longer, scared not to be with him. That fear never changed. I'm still angry with him for that fear being inside me. I still love him for his desperation, for clinging to me like I was enough to keep pretending for one more night. But it wasn't his fault alone. For two months we were both pretending. I was pretending to love him the same way I always had and he was pretending to love me differently.

I knew depression was real, but until I felt the weight of it, I underestimated its grip. I rebounded with a toxic man who eroded the world Brett and I had built together, and when we broke up it all came crashing down. I lost thirty pounds within three months. In an instant, I was disposable, and unworthy of care.

So, I just stopped.

I stopped going to my classes, I stopped eating, and I started running. It was all I could do. The thought of going to my classes, of speaking to or engaging with others horrified me. Everything I ate tasted like paint chips. Silence made me feel like I was already dead, so I played movies until I fell asleep, but I stopped listening to music because every song made me feel too much. I'd never stopped listening to music before.

One night my friend Trent came over and force-fed me blackberry jam on rice cakes. We met at the tail end of his divorce, yet I was the one crying and having food stuffed down my throat because I hadn't eaten in days. We were both split with sadness, but caring for one another lit us up again. We dealt with our grief in different ways. He clung to the hope of his wife returning to him, and I stopped eating. In moments, I wondered if our entire friendship was built on a foundation of heartbreak and self-sabotage. I'd seen it happen to other friends, and I was wary of anyone who would feed my melancholy, or demanded I feed their own. But he made me feel safe. And I tried to return the favor.

My friends were there for me in the best way they knew how, but they didn't fully understand. They were trying to love me as much as I was trying to stay alive, maybe even more. But I hadn't told them every-thing, and so they were working with only a part of me. I hadn't told them I'd been bad and that Brett had made me good. I hadn't told them about the shed and that Brett had led me away from that part of my life. I hadn't told them I had a father I loved more than anything who wasn't there because of something I could never forgive. Brett *was* me because being me was too much sometimes, something I'd forgotten until that part was ripped away.

25

I fell into my junior year of college. My life was happening with my hands on the steering wheel, and I couldn't stop remembering that Brett had been the one to teach me to how to drive in the first place. I started wearing layers upon layers of clothing, trying to hide whatever this mess was hanging from my bones. I'd spent six years measuring my physical self-esteem by a man who didn't want to have sex with women. When I awkwardly asked him about it he'd explain "being attracted to men doesn't mean the parts don't work." He went on to say that even though women could sometimes arouse him, he didn't actually desire women. What I heard was, "Yes, sometimes I can get it up. But I never actually wanted you." Because it was him, and because I'd divorced myself from my own perception of my body long ago, I heard what I thought was true. And I believed it.

By winter, I had tried and failed to find someone else to tell me what to think of my body, and went back to Fort Wayne to spend Christmas with my grandmother. She'd gotten me a Kodak digital camera, knowing I'd always loved taking pictures of my family and friends. But I'd become so isolated, I was only interested in taking photos of myself. I brought the camera back to the house I shared in Muncie with four other girls, learned to use the timer, and posed. I felt free to pose in ways I wouldn't be if the pictures were for public consumption. I posed like I was gorgeous, in outfits I no longer wore outside, and eventually, I posed for myself nude.

Once I'd uploaded the photos to my computer to get a closer look, I noticed something. Where I'd seen a woman unworthy of being desired was actually an attractive girl. My skin was clear and smooth, my breasts full and lovely, and even my stretch marks looked like an artist had drawn them just so over my hips and thighs. I couldn't stop looking at the photos. The stomach I thought came out too far looked soft and begged to be caressed.

Soon, I was obsessed. I started taking more nude photos of myself, playing with lighting, being half-clothed, and even writing things on my body. I pored over the pictures using editing software to change tints, highlighting, and shadows. Over the next semester, I fell in love with my body. I loved it the way it had always meant to be loved: ferociously and compassionately. I did not like the way I looked every day, but I loved myself.

Most of my life I've been surrounded by well-dressed women. My grandmother was a cosmetologist and seriously fashionable old lady, and her daughters followed suit. When I was small, I bent to her will easily. She could dress me however she saw fit, even when it meant I looked like a seven-year-old going on sixty. As I got older, I wanted to assert my own style, which posed a problem because I didn't have any style. Grandma would shake her head at me and say, "Someday, baby, you'll really understand how to dress. I'm just going to pray on that for you." For her, style was all about following rules. There was no room to be playful. Because I couldn't see how I fit into those rules, I refused to play the game. There was no way my mother would be able to afford to keep me decked out in trendy clothes, schedule regular hair appointments, or teach me how to use makeup she didn't wear. It doesn't take long for children to teach themselves not to want what they've already learned they won't have. I couldn't find a good enough reason to torture myself by acknowledging my futile desires for more stuff.

For many years, I just didn't try. The few times I did, for special occasions or at the behest of my grandmother, felt unnatural and like everyone could see how uncomfortable I was in my skin. Even if I looked glamorous in the moment, it seemed I was out of my body and keenly aware of everyone else's eyes on me. Being on anyone's radar because of how I looked made me feel like I was only seconds from ridicule. Even if I had no real interest in wearing the right clothes the right way, I didn't want to be made fun of for not even knowing how. Those rare moments were reminders I could dress the way they did if I wanted to. The day after, Grandma would be praying the look would stick, and I would be browsing fashion magazines lamenting my inability to put those looks together on my body.

Then I met Spencer. He was the most glamorous person I'd ever seen. The first time I met him, he was in five-inch heels and a pencil skirt, his curly brown hair dancing around the crown of his head. His makeup was minimal, like he put in effort, but knew he was already working with a better-than-solid foundation. I was walking through the atrium on our college campus when I spotted him. He was sitting alone at a table, reading, and sipping a drink in an impossibly pretty way.

I sat down beside him and said, "I'm sorry to bother you, but I think you're beautiful." He blinked his bright blue eyes several times before revealing his equally bright teeth to bless me with a smile.

"Thank you," he said, and offered his hand as if it should be kissed. My lips brushed his knuckles.

We bonded over our mutual inclination to burst into song, appreciation for good off-campus food, and an enduring love for Dr. Maya Angelou. Spencer vowed to help me feel glamorous, and I vowed to remind him how beautiful he was every chance he got. We moved in together.

Living with Spencer was like living with a human paradigm shift. He didn't just dress up or "put his face on" — he played. He didn't wear traditionally feminine clothes every day, he didn't shave every day, but he was always beautiful because he wanted to be. He introduced me to real makeup. He could make me look pretty in a thousand different ways, and still, none of them felt like me. He would go through my closet with me, picking out clothes I never wore, and forcing me to spin them into something new. Sometimes, I looked like me, but I also looked like I was trying, and I was still afraid of looking like I was trying. Even if it was fun. He did inspire me to keep searching for my look, so I did, privately and mostly only with him. Some nights, when we sat in my room, watching our favorite childhood movies, he'd tell me how cute he'd been as a child, and I would remind him how cute he still was. Then he'd ask why I couldn't be that nice to myself. Eventually, I couldn't even fake an answer, so I just stayed quiet.

For the first time, I was in a space where no one would bat an eye if I chose to play. And I played. I bought lipsticks, and watched tutorials, and let myself try things on that I assumed "didn't work for my hips." I tried filling in my eyebrows. Spencer was always there to offer help and encouragement. And tweezers, which only happened once, but emotionally, I still bear the scars.

On a trip home, I took a sweater from my grandmother's closet. It was something I loved but would have been afraid to wear before. It was black with silver buttons that clasped all the way up to my chin. The sleeves were three-quarter length and cape-like. It smelled like her. I wore it with a bright lipstick, one that was now part of "my look." I sent the video to Spencer later, and he replied with a simple and affirmative, "Yes."

26

I hadn't lived under my mother's roof in seven years, nearly to the day. We had phone check-ins every other week, with the time between calls sometimes stretching further, but never so long that I felt ignored. For the most part, the calls were fun. My mom was fun. She'd always been a good time when she wanted to be, and that had been true for as long as I could remember. Her laugh was familiar to anyone present long enough to have heard it once, and that didn't require too much time. She looked for reasons to laugh, and when she couldn't find them, she made them up herself. At any point, on any day, it was not uncommon to hear my mom giggling after her own jokes from one side of our three-bedroom ranch to the other.

It had been longer than usual since our last call, but I wasn't worried until my grandmother rang instead. I was standing in the middle of a room that wasn't mine. It belonged to the family I babysat for. Her voice came over the line and spoke words, but I was too numb to really hear anything beyond my mother being in the hospital with a ruptured appendix. I was still holding the disconnected phone in my hand what seemed like hours after my grandmother had hung up.

It struck me that if my mother died I would become some version of an adult orphan. My father was not dead, but he was unavailable to me. Did orphans have to be children? Still, if my mother died — and I was pretty sure she was dying — it seemed there should be a name for my new place in the world without her. I was not a child.

I wasn't ready to become an orphan.

The thought of my mom's laughter — the thought of never hearing it again — brought me back into the present as I stood there staring into my phone's waiting screen, trying to decide what to do with what I'd just been told. I hoped it would light up again with a simple text saying this was a mistake, a misunderstanding. My grandmother tended to exaggerate, especially in moments that were already pretty high stress. How many times had she forced my brother and me into bathtubs, covering us with a mattress to protect us from Midwestern torna- does that never touched down within a fifteen-mile radius? Didn't we constantly joke about the time she yelled, "Run! They shooting!" after a car backfired on the corner, and almost tripped my pregnant mother in the process of seeking safe refuge in the house? I felt a bit of hope. Grandma exaggerates. Everybody knows that.

I took stock of what I knew. I tried to wrestle my emotions into submission, and make sense of this situation. I knew my mother was in the hospital, and that she hadn't been well. I knew my grandmother had a tendency to make everything sound worse than it was. I also knew my grand- mother. Her voice, tired and deliberately steady, betrayed what she refused to say out loud. I thought of her words again.

When she said, "They're still trying to figure out what's going on with her," I heard, "It's not good."

"She should have come to the hospital five days ago." I heard, "It's too late."

"You should probably come see her." I heard, "Come say goodbye to your mama."

A quick Google search did nothing to ease my growing anxiety about my mother. Most of what I read were personal accounts in which the patient said the pain caused by a ruptured appendix felt as bad as giving birth or getting shot. My hand came to the place I thought my appendix might be, just to the right of my navel. Most people seek professional help immediately, the pain being too great to bear for long. And yet, when my mother's appendix burst, she lived with the pain for five days. I imagined her doubling over during the actual explosion of the sour organ inside. Her face, almost exactly like mine, but with a slightly wider nose and smaller eyes, screwed up in agony. Her body, around two hundred pounds, shapely and solid, crumpling under the weight of screaming nerve endings. I could almost see the peak of her brows reach for her hairline, her eyes widening with pain and fear. I knew the looks of my mother the way most people do: like the backs of my hands, which sometimes still surprised me with scars and moles I'd swear I'd never seen before.

It would be easy to convince someone my mother waited so long because she didn't want to miss work, or perhaps, couldn't afford to. Maybe she didn't have health insurance, and was afraid of what that the hospital bill might look like when this all turned out to be gas or something. Those would still be bad reasons not to go to the hospital, but ones easily understood, especially by anyone who has lived with (or lived through) that specific brand of economic anxiety. There's nothing like avoiding the doctor because you can't afford it, but avoiding the doctor because you don't trust them comes close. I come from a people of broken bones that were not set or cast, only weathered. A lot of that had to do with money. That was not the case with my mother. She had sick days available, and she had good insurance. If either of those reasons were why she didn't get help earlier, I might have been less angry. Or maybe not. When it comes to my mother, I have always needed less than a nudge to find myself full and hot with self-righteous anger. And when I catch myself being angry that way, I've usually found a way to blame her for that too.

When I was in the third grade, a kid in my class missed a few days because his appendix burst during recess. He and I were both playground floaters who refused to spend our precious time racing boys who pushed you down when you won, or double-Dutching with girls who pushed you down when you tripped over the rope one too many times. He and I were swingers. As soon as we'd hear the whistle that released us to play, this kid and I would run straight to the swings and start pumping our legs as hard and as fast as we could, calling out to our classmates, asking for at least one big push to get us started. My second favorite part was swinging so high the chains attached to my seat would buckle with slack in midair, and pull taut as I fell back to the world, snapping my whole body to attention and forcing my legs to sway from side to side to regain control on the way back up. My favorite part was the midair dismount. You'd only get about three good ones in before some teacher said it was unsafe, and stopped you, but this kid, on his first dismount, landed on his feet, then began to scream like he'd shattered himself inside to stick the landing.

The only male teacher on the playground scooped the kid up in his arms, and ran to the school nurse. The rest of us stood around wondering what had happened to him. As usual, the adults told us nothing. One teacher blew her whistle at those of us still standing in a circle around the place he'd once stood. "You're wasting time!" she yelled. "He's gone. Go play." I left the swings. The whistle-happy teacher now stood next to them, reaching out and grabbing those of us who were going too high or looked like we were about to jump. Of course, that meant me. I walked to the older side of the playground where I could be on my own. There were a set of monkey bars there where I liked to hang and dream. My mother said my dad liked to do the same thing when he was here, go to parks and playgrounds, lie in the grass and dream. I tried to picture him with me, but found the image tough to conjure in a real way. I didn't know what it was like to lie beside my dad in grass or anywhere else. Still, I tried to call the false memory forward. My attempt was interrupted by the sound of the teacher who'd taken the kid inside talking to another teacher about calling 911 for the nurse. I remained quiet. I wanted to hear this. The talking teacher began to cry a little, and asked his colleague, "Did you hear him scream?"

She shook her head. "No."

"I still hear it," he said. "What the fuck makes a kid scream like that?"

My mother didn't call 911. She didn't ask for help, and continued to go to work while pieces of her appendix floated off into parts of her body where doctors would never be able to retrieve them. She did this because she was afraid. Afraid of hospitals? No. Afraid of doctors? Not really. My mother was afraid that the pain searing through the middle of her body was a sign of something else, something more sinister than an infection. The demon of sickness would finally bring to fruition her worst nightmare: losing her children. My mother was afraid that she would go to the hospital, find out that she was dying, and her children would be left alone.

Orphans.

This had always been her second worst fear. The first being, of course, that one of her children would die before she did. This was the one I understood. I often awoke in the middle of the night, sweat slick from my siblings dying in nightmares. When I lived at home and had these nightmares, I would find Nikki or Jorian and slip into bed beside them. I would watch them breathe for as long as it took to settle the thump thump thumping anxiety knocking around my chest. Since we haven't lived together it's become repeated phone calls any one of them might answer by saying, "Dammit, Ashley," then hanging up, knowing their voice was all I needed to hear to comfortably return to bed. My mother's fear is similar, though perhaps more intense. This overwhelming fear nearly cost her her life, and almost made me the orphan of her nightmares. Yes, I was angry.

By the time my mother admitted to the

need for treatment, her blood was already teeming with bacteria. Septicemia, the internet informed me. Blood poisoning. Normally, people who experience septicemia can barely function due to its symptoms. I only know one other person who has ever experienced it, and he said the vomiting alone nearly drove him insane with pain. My mother was still going to work. This is how her fear had always operated. It animated her. When there was little left to motivate going through the motions of life, her fear of being judged, embarrassed, or told something is irreparably, or fatally, wrong with her body or mind, pushed her forward. In some cases, it also pushed her children away. But when you're a single parent, you take your wins and accept your losses. My mother's fear kept her children fed, clean, and housed. It kept one foot in front of the other. For the most part, up until this point, my mother's fear had assisted her in meeting her most necessary goals. She had no reason to believe it might kill her until it tried to do just that.

I called Mitch and Becky, the parents I was babysitting for, and asked if it would be okay for me to drive their two boys an hour and a half away to my hometown. I told them I wanted to check on my mother. They said of course, and asked if I needed help with anything. I told them that I would be fine, and I believed myself when I said it. Over time, this family had become my second family, filling numerous holes in parental guidance, but I was still wary. When you don't grow up with a certain kind of affection, even if you know you're worthy of it, it can be hard to accept in adulthood. I was no different than the statistics on these matters. They loved me, and I knew it. I loved them, and I knew that too. I'm pretty sure they did as well. But I could not understand their trust, or forgiveness. They were not obligated to me by blood, and so I could not fathom why or how they could love me unconditionally. I still wasn't sure if I was loved unconditionally by the people who were supposedly obligated to do so. Because I could not understand it, I could not believe it. And so, I continued to accept their love for as long as they would have me. However, for various reasons, I did not expect they would have me for long.

I packed the boys into their parents' van with snacks, toys, and a host of other distractions. They were good kids, but at five and two, still quite young. They fought sometimes, yelled sometimes, and got bored and antsy. But they were good listeners, and though I tended to hold adults to impossible standards, I seemed to have infinite patience for children. Unlike some adults, I never quit remembering what it was like to be one. Their small plights were familiar to me, as were their big feelings. I didn't feel like a child, but I felt children. These two were among my favorites.

On this trip, the boys were mostly silent. I'd told them that we were going to visit my family, my mother specifically, but I hadn't told them why. It was as if they knew I needed the quiet to think, and provided it easily without being bribed or nagged. It was a gift, purposeful or not, and I was grateful to them.

I don't remember the ride to the hospital, but I do remember our arrival into my mother's room. I knew she was sick. I had prepared to hear whatever it would be necessary for me to hear about the state of her health, her prospects, her fate. Still, somehow, in that hour and a half drive all the way there, I had not prepared to see her. My mother's gorgeous dark skin had taken on a gray pallor unlike anything I'd ever seen. Her eyes were bloodshot, and she squinted as if she were newly sensitive to the light. Her body filled the bed, but the formidable woman who raised me was missing. The woman who lay there, with my mother's name typed in small print onto the plastic band around her wrist, was dying. The formidable woman who raised me would have done no such thing. I wanted to be angry. Instead, I was deeply, startlingly sad.

"What are you doing here?" my mother asked, her voice raspy and weak. She was shocked to see me. Only then did I realize I hadn't told my grandmother, or any other member of my family, I was on my way. I'd spent half the drive there coming up with a plan for moving back and taking care of my youngest brother who was only thirteen years old, and making sure my sister wouldn't have to drop out of college. And yet, I hadn't picked up the phone and called either of them.

"I talked to Grandma," I said.

"Don't tell me what she said."

I sighed. "Okay."

The boys were small enough to sit together in the only chair in the room. From the bag I'd secretly packed, I handed them each an iPad and a Game Boy. Preemptive bribes for silence. I sat on the windowsill. My mother smiled at me, her still-recognizable smile, and I remembered to kiss her cheek. We talked for a bit. She asked how it had been babysitting the boys, and I asked about her work. I didn't reach out to her or my siblings enough, so I rarely knew what everyone had been up to. I was preoccupied with my life in my college town. I was afraid we'd grown too far apart, that my brothers and sister might not want to talk to me anyway. In our own ways, my mother and I talked to one another about our fear. Which is to say we didn't say much of anything to one another at all.

After a few minutes of our non-talking talking, a nurse popped in to tell my mother her doctor had ordered another test. Technicians would be arriving soon to move her to a lab. My mother looked terrified. She told the nurse, "My mother will be here soon. If they find anything, if they suspect anything, don't tell me. Tell my mother." The confused nurse nodded slowly, looked at me, and when she saw I had nothing more to offer than a shrug, turned on her heels and made her exit. I told my mother I'd stay until the techs arrived, and almost as soon as the words left my mouth, they did.

I kissed her graying cheeks again, and attempted an awkward hug through the rails on her bed. We both said I love you, and she told me to be safe on the road. The techs descended on her and moved fast.

They were out the door before I could finish packing up the boys and their things. By the time I turned back around, the room was empty in a way that forced me to swallow my stomach. Looking down at the unnaturally white floors didn't help. I stared at the door with a small child's hand in each of my hands. We were all quiet. For the first time in my memory, I felt like I hadn't had enough time with my mother.

As we hit the highway, the boys asked me to turn on the radio. I did, to some popular local station, and they began to sing nonsense at the tops of their lungs. It didn't bother me. It sounded like a joy I couldn't feel anymore, but sometimes, I remembered it. It made me think of my mother, who sang at the tops of her lungs every chance she got, and how this was my favorite version of her. When she sang that way, she seemed happy and unafraid. My mother wasn't perfect. Our relationship was complicated, and difficult. She was my imperfect mother. We were two different people, and found that hard to accept in one another. But I was hers and she was mine. That's how it had always been. Who would I be, if not hers? I didn't want to be without her.

It was then, on the road, with two boys screaming from the back of my borrowed van, that I promised myself I would visit my father for the first time in thirteen years. I was afraid. I could admit that. But I wasn't going to let fear kill me too.

27

After a few close calls, and two surgeries, my mother did not die. I was relieved. I was ecstatic. I could not forget her dark-gray face lit up by the dead-white hospital room, or her weak smile. I did not forget my fear of becoming parentless. I did not forget my promise.

It took mailing a five-page form and a large photocopy of my driver's license before I became an approved visitor for Indiana state prisons. Months before, my father wrote me a letter saying I was on his visitors' list. He'd written this information into every letter he'd sent me since I'd been old enough to drive. It had always seemed easy enough to do, despite the fact that I was an anxious driver. I was afraid of highways, and driving alone anywhere more than thirty minutes away scared me. Operating a vehicle is a lesson in individual control and mutual trust. I was skeptical of both.

Still, it seemed the desire to see him, to speak to him, which had been boiling over for the better part of two decades, should have been enough to get me to hit the road. It wasn't. It was the near-death of my mother.

I couldn't pinpoint one thing that kept me from visiting my father for so long. I had my suspicions, of course. Could I have been so lazy? Could he mean so little to me that I couldn't be bothered? There was some truth to both of these explanations. There is a lot of work that goes into visiting a prison, and I had no interest in doing that work. When someone you can't remember being physically involved in your life asks for physical involvement in your life, it is hard to know where and how to make room for them. I was twenty-five years old before I decided to make room for my father. The weight of this lingering choice should have shamed me. But the high of possibility, the potential for what kind of man my father might be, persisted. I did not have time to be ashamed. I was far too busy dreaming about our inevitable reunion, and his inevitable adoration of the woman his daughter had become.

After I found out I'd been approved as a visitor, I called Trent. I thought healing from our respective breakups might eventually separate us. But we were still here. Two years earlier he'd offered to take me to see my father as a Christmas present. I wasn't sure if the offer still stood, but I had to ask. I believed if I didn't ask him right then, I never would. Driving myself was out of the question. I was already nervous behind the wheel, and could vividly imagine how that nervousness might bloom compounded with the reality of seeing my father for the first time in thirteen years. It had been easier to drive to see my mother. I knew who she was, and I knew the way home. That knowledge allowed me enough comfort to feel however I needed to along the way.

There was also this: it had to be the right person. Other friends could have driven me, but I didn't want them to. It had to be someone with a nature to nurture. Someone who would deeply understand how much I would need them to be gentle with me on the way, in the moment, and especially upon our return. Truly, there was no better option.

When Trent answered the phone, I told him if he was still willing to drive me to the prison, I was ready to go. He said, "Of course. I'd love to."

The flood of relief that flowed through me was quickly replaced by anxiety. It was all working out. This was going to happen. If I wasn't ready, it was time to get ready. But I had no idea what "ready" looked like in this situation, and no one else seemed to know either. Friends made low stakes recommendations:

"You should talk to your therapist about this. A lot."

"You should write him ahead of time and make sure he knows you're coming."

"You should tell your mother you're going."

"You should take a shot of whiskey before you go in."

"Are you on antidepressants? You might want to ask about antidepressants."

"You should bring something with you that he can keep! Oh wait, can you do that?"

"Don't tell him ahead of time. Everybody loves surprises. And he probably doesn't get a lot of them."

Unfortunately (or fortunately), Trent was moving to Denver at the end of the month, so the visit had to be soon. There was no time for me to send a letter or plan much at all. The day that worked best for us both was one week away from the day I called him. My father was one week away. I thanked Trent over and over. More than once he said, "This is such a big deal. I can't believe you chose me to do this with you." I would smile up at him, and think, I wish I didn't have to make any choices ever again. This could be my last good one, and I'd be happy with that.

One week away felt sooner than it was, but I knew myself. If I had not set the wheels in motion immediately, I would have found a million and five reasons why I couldn't make the trip. No money for gas, hating the highways, not actually knowing what my father would be like when I got there. There are always excuses to be made, and I had been making them for seven years. Since I was eighteen years old, and legally able to make this trip on my own. Now I would not be alone. I'd sent in all the paperwork, and I'd asked my close friend to be my support system. I was still afraid, but I was not alone.

I'd started writing about my father that same year, what I knew of him anyway, and I couldn't stop. There was only one question that preoccupied me, kept me awake at night, and simmered under the surface of my skin like no other branch of curiosity had. This was the question I most needed answered, and the only one that couldn't possibly be answered beforehand. After thirteen years of not seeing one another face-to-face, and not hearing one another's voices, what would my father think of me?

The oldest letter I had from my father was dated in 1991. I would have been four years old, and just beginning to learn to read, but he didn't care. He had things he needed to say to me. He has been writing me for as long as I can remember. Letter upon letter filled with "I love you," "I'm proud of you," "Smile," "You're beautiful," "You're so smart," and a host of other things every young girl wants to hear from her dad. Most girls got to hear those words in person, but I thought his way was better. The most important questions were answered. Did my father love me? Yes. I had it in writing. I had it in writing over and over again.

The letters, notes, and birthday cards came all year long. I would come home from school and grab the mail right out of our box, or I would riffle through the pile my mother always set on the kitchen counter closest to the front door. Many days there were only bills, notices, or junk mail. Every once in a while, every few months or so, there would be two letters, one addressed to me and the other to my brother. The handwriting would be perfect. I would instantly be motivated to work on my chicken scratch a little harder in school, but it would never be as graceful as his. The heavier the envelope, the better. The thickness implied the inclusion of a hand-drawn card, or at the very least, a longer, more revealing message. My father was a mystery, and his letters were the clues to where I'd come from, why I was the way I was. I would take my letter to my bedroom to open privately. For many years, I did not write him back. I'm sure I had my reasons why I didn't write.

I couldn't remember any of them now.

28

The morning I left to see my father, I wore my favorite striped top and the jeans that actually fit. Nothing fancy, but still nice. I wasn't sure how he'd feel about my natural hair, but there was nothing I could do about that now, nor did I want to. I was also clearly at least twenty pounds overweight. I hoped he would look past it, that he could look past it. My beloved rhino necklace, a small token of strength, stayed on my bedside table. Visitors weren't allowed to wear jewelry. I was dressed and ready to go an hour before Trent was due to arrive. I lay on my side in bed, my hands tucked between my thighs for warmth, waiting for his text. When my phone lit up on the nightstand, I almost fell out of my bed scrambling for it. The words "I'm here!" only added to the tension coursing through my body.

I checked my bag for the fifteenth time. Driver's license? Check. Keys? Check.

Notebook to write down important thoughts in the car? Check. Valium? I wished.

I met Trent at the bottom of the stairs. He pulled me into a hug, and breathed into my hair for a moment. My charging heart stilled a bit, just enough for me to take a deep breath, the first one of the day.

When he released me from the calming embrace, he grabbed my hand. "Thank you so much for letting me do this for you, Ashley." When we got to his car, there was a flower sitting on the seat for me.

Halfway there he asked when was the last time I saw my father, and I told him it'd been thirteen years.

"Has he had any visitors since then?" I rolled down the window, and considered his question.

"I don't know. I hope so." I kept my face just outside the window frame, allowing the air to whip around my nose, mouth, and closed eyes. It reminded me of being a child and jumping off the swings at the playground. Even when I was scared, I wouldn't open my eyes. Sometimes I landed poorly, but it felt better that way.

Trent spoke again. "Thirteen years is a long time not to see anybody you love."

I rolled the window back up.

"I don't think it's been thirteen years." I

didn't know if this was true, but I hoped. It was one thing not to see your father for thirteen years. It was quite another for him not to have seen one familiar face in thirteen years. If I was going to be the first loving face he saw in over a decade, I wished I had a perfect face.

The drive to the prison was shorter than I thought it'd be, or hoped it'd be. Only about an hour and a half. The facility looked the way you'd expect a prison to look. Everything was a flat concrete gray and a sickening yellow-leaning beige. Trent dropped me off at the door. Waiting in the parking lot wasn't allowed, so he'd have to find someplace to hang out by himself in the middle of nowhere.

I rummaged around in my bag for all my quarters. I'd brought ten dollars' worth. I knew you could bring change for the vending machines, and sometimes you could use them to take a picture with your loved one. I wanted a picture more than I wanted anything else. The only photo I had of myself with my father was thirteen years old. I also wanted to be able to buy him a cookie. R.C. had always had an insatiable appetite for sweet things. If you brought a treat into the house, you'd better hide it, or he would find it and eat it without remorse.

When we were younger my mother would shake her head and say, "Just like your daddy, you and these sweets."

My mother never said anything bad to us about our father, but over the years she talked about him less and less. I assumed it was because she'd run out of things to say. They hadn't been married for very long before he went to prison. Maybe she'd told us everything she knew. I didn't know what it meant to have a broken heart. I was unfamiliar with longing and despair. It did not resonate with me that the father I'd never really known was also the husband she lost. I did not know that there are miles between running out of things to say, and running out of the strength to say them.

Still trying to leave Trent's car, nervousness radiated around me. I kept dropping the quarters, starting to leave the car, then stopping to check and make sure I had everything I needed again. It was as if I'd thrown my momentum out the window somewhere along the road. It didn't feel right. It felt sudden. I was still afraid, I still had questions, and I wasn't sure I could make it out of the car with everything I needed. Trent leaned over and placed his steady hand over mine. I looked toward him, and he smiled.

"It's going to be good. You've waited a long time for this. Tell him I said hello."

Again, my heart stilled. I put all the quarters in my pocket and finally stepped out of the car. My chest tightened on the walk to the door, but I remembered to breathe deeply. The waiting room was full of foot-tapping visitors. The chairs looked like the hard plastic Fisher-Price furniture that gets passed down over and over in working-class families. As soon as your cousins were too big for it, ta-da! You just inherited some bite-sized kiddie furniture perfect for playing pretend, and not messing up your mother's good table when you ate. Its blue-gray coloring looked dirty to me.

The two officers working the sign-in booth were busy doing a job made for more than just two people, and they knew it. Don't be any trouble, and you'll be fine. Internally, my pep talks were thin and already guilt-ridden. I was certain I would do something to mess this up for my father and me. As I stuffed my bag into a locker that cost me four of my quarters, I checked and rechecked to make sure I hadn't forgotten my ID. I hadn't. But I checked again.

In the long line to add your name to the waiting list, I watched a woman get frustrated with the officers. She'd brought her cell phone into the facility and apparently, that was not allowed. It wasn't just something you couldn't take into the visiting room, it was something you weren't allowed to have in the building at all. She would have to walk it back to her car, then come back in and find a place at the end of the line again. It was only then that I noticed the signage all around the room.

NO CELL PHONES ALLOWED ON PREMISES!

LEAVE CELL PHONES IN YOUR CAR!

YOU MAY BE ASKED TO LEAVE IF CELL PHONE FOUND ON YOUR PERSON!

My fingers twitched toward the cell phone I'd forgotten to silence in my pocket. I prayed it wouldn't ring while I was so close to giving the officers my father's and my names. When I got to the front of the line, I answered every question quickly, then raced back to my locker to silence and hide my phone. I would have taken it out to the parking lot except that Trent wouldn't be there, and if I left the waiting room, I might miss them call my name. I considered burying it in the gravel on either side of the sidewalk and just digging it out when I was done with my visit. Instead, I just sat and wondered if they'd search the lockers while

I was talking to my dad, if they'd pull me out of our reunion because I hadn't noticed the signs about the cell phones until it was too late. I pictured myself being grabbed by the officers and dragged away from him. I knew it was terribly dramatic, but I couldn't shake the image. The other picture in my mind was of my dad, fighting them all, eyes blazing, warning them through clenched teeth, "Take your hands off my daughter."

I felt worried, and proud, and protected thinking of it. Despite everything my father had done, I was still so eager to be claimed by him. To be protected by him. To the world he was a bad man. To me, he was my dad who did a bad thing. I was still trying to figure out what it meant to love someone who had done such a bad thing, but I did love him. And that was enough for me to show up, and say so to his face.

I couldn't sit, so instead, I paced. I counted backward from one hundred. I picked at my clothes so much I thought they might check me for fleas before they allowed me inside. I jumped when they called my father's last name, my last name. It was time to go in for my visit. I went through the pat-down and the metal detector. Then the female officer asked the male officer if I was allowed to wear my headband in. He shook his head. She said I'd have to put it back in my locker, and get back in line. I took it off and handed it to her.

"Just throw it away."

". . . are you sure?"

"Absolutely."

She looked at me like I might be a nut job, and threw it away in the garbage can at her feet. In that moment, I didn't care what my father thought of the way I looked. I wanted him to see me. She handed me a plastic tub for my shoes, belt, and quarters, then opened the big heavy door in front of me. I walked through, putting my belt and shoes back on after the door closed behind me. When I'd gathered the last of my quarters from the bin, a second large door opened for me to enter. I held my breath and stepped inside.

Once I entered the room, I scanned the crowd of tables for my father. I'd stared at the few pictures I had of him enough to recognize him anywhere. I was no longer that little girl sitting on my grandmother's bed not knowing who her daddy was. His face was burned into my brain as much as my own.

Another officer directed me to a log sheet. I signed my name quickly, nearly dropping the pen. My hands were shaking. By the time I turned back around, my dad was standing up.

My tears came swiftly. My first instinct was to run to him, but I was mindful enough to realize that running in a prisoner visitation room might be on the list of Shit You Don't Do in a Prison.

I walked calmly, if eagerly, toward him. He held his arms wide open and smiled. Then, I sprinted. My right cheek landed directly in the middle of his chest. He squeezed me tightly and kissed the top of my head, my forehead. He knew me. He whispered into my hair, "I love you, I love you, I love you . . ."

There was his voice. It was deep and sincere. It made so much sense why I loved talking to my uncle Clarence, my father's younger brother, so much. They sounded almost identical.

"I love you too, Daddy."

I'd told myself before I got there, that I would refer to him as "Dad" because I was not a child. I was a grown woman, and I was pretty sure grown women didn't call their fathers "Daddy." But in that moment, I felt like someone's little girl. And I'd been waiting a long time to feel like somebody's daughter.

He walked me to our seating area. He

looked at me and smiled. He was handsome. I look so much like him. Much more so in person than in pictures. It was startling, and familiar, and I promised myself that I would make it a memory. I would not forget how this felt, to notice how much I looked like my father. To feel this sameness in our blood, and countenance, and capacity for love.

My father loved me as much in person as he did in his letters. Maybe even more. He held my hands as long as he was allowed, which was five minutes for every thirty minutes. He spoke to me softly, as if the full volume of his emotions might scare me away. It quickly became apparent that he was trying to put his best foot forward as much as I was trying to do the same. We were in awe and terrified of one another. He leaned toward me, his words low and hesitant.

"I could sit here and stare at you all day, Ashley. But we ain't got but a couple of hours. Let's talk."

"Okay." I thought about every question I'd wanted to ask him, important and poignant questions. Instead, I said, "What have you been up to?"

I regretted the question immediately. I had asked a man who had been in prison for twenty-four years the unabridged version of "What's up?" I assumed it made me look dumb, or worse, uninteresting. My father smiled.

"Not much today, but I've been up to a few things here or there since the last time I saw you."

He filled me in quickly. While incarcerated he'd earned two degrees, an associate's in art and a bachelor's in business. He read voraciously. He was a funny guy. Really funny. Inside, that's what he was known for: scholarship, art, and his sense of humor. And he loved me. He loved me and my brother and my mother. He missed us. He drew us all the time. He had photos of us taped to the wall in his cell. Sometimes, he said, we were the only thing keeping him alive.

I was the first person to visit him in five years. His father, my Grandpa J, had attempted to visit him five years earlier and had suffered a heart attack behind the wheel. Since then, there'd been no one. Not his brothers, his sister, cousins, aunts, uncles, or his children. The love he hoped we had for him sustained him though he could not see it. He looked around to see where the guards were standing, and when he was certain the coast was clear, he grabbed my hands again. My father is one of the few people I know whose hands are bigger than mine.

"I knew it was you."

"What do you mean?"

"When they told me I had a visitor, they couldn't say who it was, but I knew. If anybody loved me enough to come into this hellhole, it would be my baby girl."

The first question he asked me was, "Is my daughter happy?" because that was what was most important to him. I said, yes, because it was mostly true. The parts of my life that weren't happy, I wasn't ready to talk about. Not with him. Not yet. There was nothing he could do about them, and I hadn't yet figured out if there was something I could do about them.

My father and I sat and talked for two hours and forty-seven minutes about anything we could think of in the moment. We covered politics (both of us were progressive), religion (he believed in God, I didn't), and even relationships (we were both happily single). I asked him about his relationships before he married my mother. He told me that he had been in love with someone else before he met my mother, but it was complicated. He would tell me more in a letter.

I laughed more than I cried, but I did cry. He sneakily held my hands here and there. He spoke to me with the weight of a sincerity I'd never known; it frightened me. In every story he told, I could tell he had been waiting to say those exact words to me for thirteen years, perhaps longer. He'd thought it through, what kind of conversation he would want to have with me. He'd maybe even practiced. He knew I would come, and he would not let himself be so overwhelmed that he could not say all that he wanted to say. We were alike, my father and I.

After telling a joke about the man he shared a cell with, a joke that made me laugh from the center of my belly, my father got serious and quiet.

"Do you need anything from me, Ashley? Anything at all? I know I can't do much from here, but if you need something, I'll do whatever I can to get it to you."

My voice caught in my throat, then I coughed up the question I needed to ask.

"I've been writing about you. Well, really about me. But a lot of it has to do with how I feel about you. But not just you. Actually, it's about me being a kid, a little girl, and all the stuff that goes with that. And I use passages from some of your letters when I write about what they mean to me, or how they made me feel. Is that okay? Me writing about you? I don't want to stop."

He put his hand up to stop me from explaining. He sat back in his chair, and released a breath that caused his whole body, shoulders down, to sink farther into his baggy tan uniform.

"When you sent me one of your stories, I thought, damn. I must be the luckiest fool in the world. I got me a daughter who's smart, beautiful, and she's a writer. A real one. A good one. I'm so proud of you, Ashley."

"Thanks, Daddy." I stared at my palms, unable to look him in the eye. He sat forward, and without looking around, put his palm in mine.

"So, look, I don't know what all you're writing, and maybe it don't make me sound too good, but that's not your fault. That's on me. This is something I can give you if you need it. You need my permission? You got it."

I looked at him. I don't know what I'd expected. I guess I hadn't even expected to ask him that particular question, but his permission gave me direction.

"Hands off!" A guard glared at my father, and he released my hands, mumbling under his breath.

"These muthafuckas . . . I'm trying to talk to my daughter."

I did not want to think of my father as a violent man, though his incarceration was the result of his capacity for violence. I wanted to believe that had he been a free man, he would have been a fierce guardian, and I wouldn't have ever been forced to endure all the times I couldn't bring myself to tell him about. I couldn't reconcile these two desires. I thought I would have learned by now.

The machine used to take pictures was broken, so we didn't get to take a photo. I wasn't ready to leave when we were told our time was up. I couldn't imagine how I would ever be ready to leave. There was still so much to say.

My father and I hugged. He walked me to the front of the visiting room. He squeezed me one last time and sat in the designated seat for prisoners to return to wherever they came from on the inside. Separate from the rest of us. Separate from me. In most cases, I was glad to be separated from the dangerous criminals I saw on the news and in the papers. This day, it felt cruel.

I waited in the line of people leaving their loved ones, most of us weeping. I turned frequently to look back and wave at him as he waited. He was always smiling, staring at me, waiting to wave back. There in case I needed him. I was turning back for the umpteenth time when he said my name. He opened his mouth, then closed it again. He wanted to say something he hadn't prepared.

"Do me a favor, Ashley? When you write about you and me? Just tell the truth. Your truth. Don't worry about nobody's feelings, especially not mine. You gotta be tough to tell your truth, but it's the only thing worth doing next to loving somebody."

I nodded through my tears.

"Okay, Daddy."

Just then, the door opened and the visitors began filing into another world, the outside world. I turned and blew him a kiss. He pretended to catch it. That was the first time I got to blow my father a kiss, and he pretended to catch it. *I must remember this,* I thought. I turned the corner, passed the last window I could see him through. As soon as he was out of my line of sight, I panicked. I ran back to the glass window, still crying. He was in the seat, smiling, waiting for me.

I mouthed, "I love you."

He laughed, and I wished I could hear it, just one more time. He mouthed, "I love

292

you too. Now go!"

I waved one last time and rounded the corner.

I got three hours to tell the person I loved who I was, now I had to gather my quarters and head back to my life, separate from him.

It felt wrong to walk out of that ugly building without my father. I wanted to be taking him away from there. It felt wrong not to be holding his hand and heading home together. I was in no position to pardon him for the crimes he hadn't committed against me, and I didn't want to be. I could not forgive him in place of those he had harmed.

I wept all the way to Trent's car. He was breaking the law and waiting there for me, sleeping, and unafraid of being caught. I opened the passenger door, and he stirred awake.

"How did it go?"

I opened my mouth to answer, and instead, I dissolved. In the visiting room, there was no space to break down, to melt with emotion. Sitting across from my father for the first time in thirteen years, both of us swollen with all the things we needed to say to one another, the thought of letting all of this feeling overtake me seemed wasteful. Inefficient. In those moments, I needed more from myself. Restraint. But now, I was

293

in a car with one of my closest friends. The visit was over. Every little thing I couldn't allow myself to feel in my father's presence made itself known.

Trent rubbed my back. "What can I do?"

After I caught my breath, I answered. "A drink. I need a drink."

Trent laughed, and mentioned that he'd spotted a winery on our way there. We should pop in and see if we could do a tasting. I agreed.

As we pulled off, Trent asked, "Did you get what you needed?"

I rolled down the window again, and closed my eyes.

"Yes, I think I did."

"How does that feel?"

I smiled to myself. My father's permission to keep writing felt like a secret I wasn't ready to tell. I leaned farther out the window. I could hear the wind zipping past the planes of my face, still tight and sticky with tears I hadn't bothered to wipe away. The sunshine turned the inside of my eyelids pink and purple. Inside of myself, I let go. I did not worry about what I hadn't been able to share, or the life I was returning to. For half a minute, I was flying. For half a minute, I knew I had it in me to tell the truth, and be loved anyway.

29

After visiting my father, I never really shifted into my senior year. The cost was too much, and I couldn't sustain the scramble to make ends meet while affording tuition at the same time. I stayed in Muncie, taking a class at a time to cut costs and lingering in spaces generally reserved for students.

I met a few friends at a bar called Savages downtown. The two-dollar beers there were enough to get me tipsy without making me feel bad for buying good drinks I couldn't ever finish. I found my friends in the winterized sunroom section and sat down to shoot the shit or wait to shoot pool. Somehow the subject of the locals came up, and we started to question at what point someone who lives here but never seems to graduate or stop taking classes officially becomes a townie. Townies was a term I'd seen used to start fights and describe the nicest guy in the room. But even people who used it in a non-pejorative sense didn't want to be called one. I realized I was closing in on all the criteria.

One of the guys leaned toward me and said, "You're going to be like . . . the Kim Kardashian of Muncie."

He laughed, but I didn't.

The first thing I did when I walked into my bedroom that night was write on the chalkboard wall beside my desk, "Get out of here as fast as you can." Muncie hadn't been all bad to me by any means. I'd found close friends who felt like family, a real passion for writing, and a creative community who supported my work, and often, just me. The father of the boys I'd babysat, Mitch, and his wife, Becky, were two of them. "I think you're done with this place, kiddo." He'd stopped me for a hug in the front yard, and just when I thought he was going to let go, he held me tighter and said, "No matter where you go, this home will be yours." I cried openly while walking to my car. It hurt, wanting him to be right.

Fort Wayne was the most reasonable option to move. I even had an offer to stay with a friend from high school, rent-free, while her husband was deployed. It would mean being able to attend my little brother's football games, and my sister's track meets at the local college. I knew more people there than anywhere else in the world. My mother's and my relationship was still rocky, but I constantly worried I wasn't spending enough time with my family. I was also afraid to go back and live there again. I was different, and not everybody was going to be able to handle that, and I didn't trust myself to handle them.

I found myself looking for a way out, and when an old friend called and asked if I'd like to move into his third bedroom in Indianapolis, I said "Yes, hold it for me. I'll be there." Like every move before, I quickly decided what could fit into my car, and what couldn't. Everything that didn't fit would have to be given away, thrown away, or abandoned. No one was going to pull up with a U-Haul or a larger vehicle and help me, and I didn't think to ask for help. I stuffed my Ford Taurus to the gills, and hit I-69 for Indianapolis, leaving behind a few precious things, trying to forget them along the way.

To make rent, buy gas, and eat food I worked two jobs, one as an after-school tutor for children in Indianapolis homeless shelters, and another down the road as the part-time receptionist in the administrative office of a church. I was also getting small freelance assignments from a local copy-writing agency. It was easy, boring, and it paid. Copywriting in my cold, sun-drenched bedroom didn't require the patience of wrangling small chronically neglected children, nor the fortitude to listen to a midfifties divorcée go on a rant about her ex-husband. None of it was particularly rewarding. Half of my tutoring groups were made up of children who read at or exceeded their grade level, and in the other half I was teaching seven-year-olds the alphabet. I couldn't help any of them as much as I wanted to. And spending time around people who work on the business side of church — yes, there's a business side — was a great way to remember why church never made sense to me, even when I begged God to make it so.

After a couple months of working nonstop, I still didn't have anything close to the amount of money I would need to finish my last college requirements. When I froze and allowed myself to consider it may all have been for nothing, that I was never going to reach the heights that were expected of me, the ensuing panic shook me loose from my numbing place and pushed me toward something new. That anxious kick-start always came when I was most in need of assistance, but it was becoming harder and harder to access. The panic that used to help me jump up and finish a paper overnight could only be activated by something as dire as meeting a basic need. Even then, at times, my motivation couldn't break through. I needed something else.

Shuffling through a lackluster and inconsistent morning routine, I was late to every job I had except copywriting. I knew I'd get in trouble, and apologized profusely to my superiors when called on it, but I didn't stop. I couldn't convince myself that my presence mattered, and so found it harder and harder to show up. Sometimes, speeding down Central Avenue on my way to work, I'd remind myself that I couldn't fuck this up. I didn't have anything or anyone to fall back on. If I got fired, I was on my own. Or worse, I'd have go backward. *Is that what you want?* I asked myself, knowing the answer.

No, I didn't want to go back, not to any of the places I'd already been. Then why did I keep missing meetings, losing paperwork, and being late? When I asked myself, *What if you fail?* My brain answered, *Isn't that what you're already doing?* I felt it wasn't true, but I couldn't find the arguments to defend myself.

Maybe you can't find them, because they aren't there. Maybe that was true. I didn't want it to be. It felt wrong. And yet.

My grandmother's comforting laugh came through the phone when I called to complain. It made me miss her, her warm house, and every delicious meal she'd ever made just for me. When she asked how I'd been doing, I told her I was on the verge of being fired. "Well," she said. "You know you can al—"

"Don't," I said. She huffed like I had my nerve, and it was true, I did. It was never my intention to hurt or frustrate my grandmother, but it felt so important she know, that all my family know, I was not coming back because I was not the same person, and I could not, would not pretend. Really it was for their own good. I complicated the narrative they wanted to live by, and it didn't bother me until it bothered them. I didn't want to run from my family. I wanted to be who I was, and I didn't know if that person fit among them anymore. I was afraid to find out that I wouldn't. My lessons hadn't always come the way I wanted or hoped, but I was not ashamed of how I had changed, and I was determined to remember that. Sometimes, when I was with my family, I forgot.

"You need to go to the library," my grandmother offered. "Remember when you spent so much time at the one up here?"

The library's front door was across the road from mine, and I dutifully followed my grandmother's instructions. I hadn't lived this close to a library since I was a child, and I checked out book after book. I got weird looks from the white librarians as I pulled different books from the shelves. The librarians I'd grown up around had been white too, but they hadn't seemed afraid of me or anyone else. I suppose I was a child then, not a woman who spent three hours in their facility in the middle of the day, book-browsing, wandering through the aisles, and touching the spines as I read them for titles, authors, and interest. It didn't matter that I knew I loved these volumes now the same way I did then because the people who looked at me didn't think I looked like that might be true.

Truthfully, I'd been reading for school, or to keep up with conversation for a long time. It felt good to read toward answers to the questions in my head, a familiar source of solace I hadn't tapped in too long. It made me miss home even though I didn't want to be there. I started to miss my father, who wrote to me about the books he was reading. I never wrote back — I still didn't know what to say or how to confront what he'd done. But I found him in the pages I skimmed through. I'd pushed down the thought of him for such a long while, but he was always there in the background. A nagging thought demanding my attention, telling me how good and smart I might be, more so than I realized, and how much more I might be worthy of. Like a better story.

30

It wasn't lost on me that I mostly spoke my truth in the spaces where my family was absent. Still, the words for an essay about what had happened to me in the shed, about discovering why my dad was in prison, and how it made me feel, poured out. There was small comfort in knowing my mother could barely use email, let alone browse the Internet for my writing. I planned to post the essay to a blog I shared with some writer friends from college, having no idea the response it would get. Still, I knew I should tell her. When the essay went up, my mother would know what had happened to me in her backyard, and that I hadn't come to her like I promised I would.

It rained all day, but when I went out on our front porch, just after dark, the rain had stopped. The wet asphalt shimmered under the streetlights like it was covered in broken glass. I called my mother to confess.

We greeted each other, and she told me about a recent football game of my baby brother's. It astounded me how much she knew about the game, how closely she followed his stats, and her commitment to being in the stands almost every time he played. Even away games. The youngest was giving her the chance to mother the way she wanted, and in some ways, it made her vulnerable. I stepped off the porch, and paced on the sidewalk in front of the apartment.

"Mom," I said. "I'm writing an essay, and there's something in it I want you to know before you read it." My words sucked every bit of mirth out of the atmosphere between us.

"What?" She said it hard, flat, less like a question and more like a demand.

I remembered that I was not my little brother, and their dynamic had nothing to do with me. But I still had something to say.

"I was raped." I said it, and left it there.

"It was Bradley, wasn't it?" she said it like she'd been there in the shed with me. Like she'd already known. "I understand why you didn't tell me."

I stopped pacing, and held my breath. I didn't know what to say, and I was scared

304

to say more.

My mother spoke instead. "I was crazy back then."

The essay went up, and then it was republished in a literary magazine, and people wrote to me from all over about my work. My writing.

The piece landed me a job as an administrative assistant at a small company in Indianapolis, and my life miraculously began to stabilize. When bill collectors called regarding past-due medical and credit card bills, I was able to offer them some form of payment, or take on payment plans knowing I would actually be able to meet the obligations. When my friends wanted to go out to celebrate a birthday, or meet up at a bar for no reason at all, I now had enough money to cover my own meal, drink, and add to the tip. I signed up for health insurance, and twice a week I took myself out for dinner. On Sundays, I bought flowers and arranged them on the coffee table. I looked at them and thought about my father, and how his hands had held mine while he emphatically told me to write our story. I thought about how beautiful living things, cut off from their joy, eventually wither and die. Then I pushed that thought from my mind.

For me, this was the dream. A stable, full-time, non-demanding position that paid enough to afford a small life and still allowed me to write on the side. It's what I was working toward those last two years of college, and what I'd come to Indianapolis to find. A writer friend named Isaac had even offered to link me up with people looking for writers in New York City, which sounded like another world. I didn't really believe him, but the offer made me feel good.

I knew I was lucky to have so many people rooting for me, good people and writers who were on my side, but sometimes my feelings of unworthiness crept in. A part of me was ashamed that I'd gotten my version of "it all," and felt compelled to smash it under my heel.

During my lunch breaks at work I would walk around the neighborhood just behind the main drag. Just as I had as a child, I made up stories about the people who must live in those houses, and tried to ignore the gathering anxiety in the center of my chest. It made me angry. I didn't want to be sad, I didn't want to be anxious, I didn't want to want anything more than I had. *Enough.* I tried to settle my spirit on my own. *What more could you need? Will any of it be enough?*

I waited for my nerves to trip the numbing wire, but the warm nothing never came. I started to panic on the sidewalk, anxiously looking around me, not for help, but to make sure no one was watching this happen. The sweat forming in the palms of my hands loosened my grip on my phone, reminding me it was there. I could call someone. My fingers started moving, and soon I heard my mother's voice.

"Hello, Daughter!" I could tell she was suppressing a smile, pleased that I had called her.

"Hello, Mother," I responded, matching her tone. Then I started crying, and for a whole minute, I didn't stop. When I spoke again, I told my mother I was sorry for crying, but I just didn't feel happy, and I didn't know what to do. "It's a great job, Mama. I don't know. I just feel like I'm supposed to be doing something else even though I should feel grateful for this."

"What makes you happy?"

I stopped walking. Had she ever asked me that before? I assumed the only time my mother had ever missed me was after I'd moved out of her house, and even that took a whole year. Somewhere along the way, somewhere in all that time of hasty, inconsistent phone calls and one-way visits, my mother started to warm to me. Our conversations became easier, and I found a deep and resounding comfort in having the choice to walk away when they went to places I didn't want them to go, or didn't trust myself to come back from. But now, I didn't want to walk away. I wanted to give her a true answer.

"I like . . . making things. Art. Stories. I want to write." I wondered if she knew, when I said I wanted to write, that I meant I wanted to write about me, about us, about everything I saw, and believed, and thought I might know.

She let out a breath. "Ashley, you're the only person who has to live in your skin, and wake up with the consequences of your choices. That's why you can't let other people make the big choices for you. You have to do what it feels right to do, and you can't let anybody stop you." I heard the stifled smile again. "Not even me."

Isaac hadn't been kidding when he said he wanted to connect me with a few editors at the media company where he worked. Within a month, I'd gotten emails from and pitched two of them. Both pitches were accepted, and the first called for me to mention my history with sexual harassment and assault. It didn't mention my father's story, but my own, and the aftermath of knowing the reality of violation in your body, and keeping it there so nobody else could see it. I wanted to write about it. I used to buckle under the shame of what had happened to me in that shed, but my anger outweighed my sadness the more I talked and wrote about what happened.

Everything moved at a pace I wasn't accustomed to, and I welcomed it. Within three months I was accepted into a writer's residency, rekindled an old flame from college, and got offered a full-time writing position for a growing media publication in Manhattan. Kelly and I started seeing each other casually toward the end of our time at Ball State, but he wasn't meant to be a romantic love, or at least, I didn't mean for him to be. He was three years younger than me, the kind of party boy I found it hard to keep up with, and he was leaving at the end of the semester for an internship in New York City. When his internship ended, he came back to Indiana for a bit, then landed in Seattle. He kept calling me. One day, he called me to say he was in Indianapolis and wanted to see me. About one week later, we decided he was my boyfriend, and he returned to Seattle. I was certain he'd break up with me upon learning I'd accepted a job that would keep us even farther apart, but he sighed and said, "I guess I'll meet you in the city."

Before I moved, I drove up to Fort Wayne to see friends and family, part of a pre-move farewell tour. When I called my mother to tell her I was coming, she mentioned that my grandmother had not been feeling well, and had been admitted to the hospital. Her tone of voice, higher and lighter than usual, didn't inspire the confidence she obviously intended. My stomach sank to my feet at a snail's pace, and landed just as I crossed the city limits.

My grandmother was sleeping when I walked into her hospital room, an old friend dozing in the chair next to her bed. When I softly said hello to them both, my grandmother's friend rose with a start, snorted, and began her goodbye before she was on her feet. She reached out to me for a hug, then leaned over my grandmother for a farewell air kiss. She didn't really like to be touched in the best of times, and this woman knew her well enough to know she'd like it even less now. I panicked at the thought of being alone with my grandmother — something I'd never felt before — and assured her small, slow-moving friend she was welcome to stay.

"No, thank you, baby," she demurred. "I already slept through half of my next visit!" She picked up her open bible from the table beside her, and said goodbye again. Then she stopped, turned back to the bed, and reached out to hold my grandmother. The hug they shared lasted long enough to make me think I was right to hesitate. My grandmother didn't hold people. She didn't lean into anyone's arms. I'd never seen my grandmother be held. And so, I suspected, almost immediately, I would not have long to ever see it again. After she left, I turned to take the friend's seat. The chair was still warm from her slumbering body. I sank in, and soaked it up. My hands were already beginning to tremble.

My grandmother and I caught up for about five minutes before going silent. I stared at her, and she stared at the television set near the foot of her bed. In a moment, she picked up the remote control to change the channel, clicking toward something in black-and-white, something with a little more dust. I assumed she was looking for what felt most like home to her, and less like the room we currently shared. She settled on an on old favorite, *Bonanza.* She didn't turn her eyes away from it when she said, "It's cancer."

I covered her hand with mine. I felt the cold steel of the hospital bar beneath my fingers and her palm. My stomach churned with fear, and my torso threatened to fold over into the familiar ball I became when I thought my feelings could shoot from the soft core of my body, exploding from intensity, and destroying me from the inside out. The tears I felt coming stopped just before springing from their hiding places. My mind raced with anxious thoughts, sadness, and then, resolve.

She turned her head toward me at half speed. She looked into my eyes and said, "I don't want to do chemotherapy."

I leaned close enough for my grandmother — my dearest love — to hear the smile I couldn't bring to my face. "Then you don't have to."

Billie Coles was going to die. Like everything else she had ever done or said, it would be done her way. After all she had given me, despite whatever cruelties had snuck in along the way, I owed her my willingness to walk beside her during this time. I would hold her hand.

"I think I'll stay in Indiana a little longer."

I said it before I thought it. I couldn't say why — I knew I didn't want to stay in Indiana or tell the people in New York City I would no longer be coming. The dream I'd worked toward was so many miles away, and nothing inside me wanted to give it up. But this was my grandmother. Hadn't she held and protected me when no one else had? Taken me away to the farm, let me choose my own movies, and bought me a toy every single Saturday for almost a year? Hadn't she doted on me, and made me feel loved? All she'd ever really asked for was my company and willingness to listen. This was the best I had to offer. My dreams in exchange for a debt owed.

My grandmother turned to me with flared nostrils. "Hell, no you won't. Just call."

Her gaze returned to the television. I was both relieved and disgusted at myself for the heft of my relief. I would call. I would check on her. I would defend her and her decisions until her last breath. As I sighed and relaxed my already rising shoulders, I began to count her breaths. One . . . two . . . three . . . four . . . five . . . six . . . seven. I counted and I wondered, despite the thought's morbidity, how many inhales and exhales she had left to go.

We sat like that, in silent agreement about

our roles moving forward, for another hour. Before I left, I bent down and kissed my grandmother's cheek. Her skin was soft like the brushed underside of a leather belt. She smelled like powder, and musk, and sweat, but somehow, not at all like the hospital. I took a deep breath, hoping to keep the scent with me, as I left the room.

Two weeks later, I walked into the Indianapolis Airport with all my belongings packed into two bags. I headed straight for security. The TSA agent looked at my driver's license and asked how long I would be visiting New York. I looked at him with determination, responding that I was not a visitor, I was a future resident.

He scanned my face, then looked me up and down skeptically. "Okay, how long will you be staying in New York?"

I stood up as tall as my body would let me. "As long as they want me." It was the kind of thing you can only get away with saying in the Midwest, so I said it before I was gone too far away.

My flight went smoothly, and Brett met me at LaGuardia. He carried my bags into the taxi line, then helped the driver get them into the trunk. He'd moved to New York to give Broadway his best shot almost six months before I arrived. When I told him I was coming, he squealed and insisted he'd meet me. He didn't allow me to argue — he wasn't new.

It had been a long time since we last saw each other, and he was involved with someone now. I was happy for him. It took time, but we'd learned how to have one another without a romantic element. He helped me into the back of the taxi, slid into the seat next to mine, and gave the driver directions to Isaac's apartment, where I would be staying for two weeks. He kissed my cheek and fell asleep on my shoulder.

After Brett helped me pull my two duffel bags into Isaac's apartment, he bid me farewell and made his way back to Washington Heights. I sank into a yellow armchair and closed my eyes. My phone rang. It was my mother. I smiled at her calling, checking up on me, and felt a little embarrassed at the inner flit of glee. It seemed so normal. I answered the call.

"Hello, Mother," I said. She didn't greet me back in our usual way, so I sat up a little.

"I have a question," she said.

"Of course, you can ask me a question." I heard her stop moving on the other end. This was starting to feel more like an interrogation than a check-in. She finally spoke.

"Why can't you ever write about the happy times we had? We had happy times too." I closed my eyes, let my head fall back onto the chair, and suppressed a smile even though there was no one else around to see it.

31

I wasn't in New York long before my sister called to tell me our grandmother was in the hospital again. I told her I'd be home as soon as I could. After we hung up, I realized I couldn't actually afford the airfare. I'd moved out of Isaac's apartment, and in with Kelly. We were paying two-thirds of the monthly rent to live in the smaller room of a two-bedroom apartment. He'd just started working through a temp agency, but his first check hadn't come in yet, and even when it did, we would need it — all of it — just to keep our bills paid. Eventually, a generous mentor and friend offered to pay for my flight home. Where I would usually put up a fight, feeling unworthy of such an act of care, I humbly accepted. For my grandmother, even at her worst, I would have asked each person I met for a dollar until I had every cent I needed to say goodbye.

Pulling into the visitors' parking lot, I

remembered how hospitals made me feel. The hallways were stark and busy. All the white, the quick tapping, and furtive small movements reminded me of too many mice in a maze. Everything that happened here felt secretive, as if sickness and death were, or should be, a person's great shame. Things moved quickly and deliberately, but you were just supposed to pretend none of it was happening. Just don't look. Just smile at the nurse through your tears. Just visit the gift shop. Just grab a coffee in the cafeteria. Just forget this feeling, and decide to be somewhere else in your mind, especially if that place doesn't include sickness, injury, disability, or death. If you have to be here, be somewhere else too. I was familiar with those rules, but had run away from them a long time ago. I was out of practice.

Instead of writing down my grandmother's room number, I'd memorized it. I didn't trust myself not to lose a piece of paper, or to find a note I'd made in my phone. This was a moment where I'd have to trust my ability to make a memory and keep it. For her, I could do this.

When I walked up to the nurse's station, and asked to see Billie Coles in room —, the nurse gave me a sad smile before pointing toward a plain brown door and telling me where I would need to turn right or left. I rushed past a visitors' lounge where members of my family sat playing with a few cousins, nieces, and nephews. Everyone was here, but my body compelled me to go only in the direction the nurse had told me to, lest I lose the memory, and so, lose my way. My back was straight and I knew every step toward her room could be the step when I began to hear the cries that would tell me I was too late. My anxiety propelled me forward. Standing still was not an option.

When I found the door to my grandmother's hospital room, I whipped back toward the visitors' lounge, suddenly needing a moment to think before I saw her. Knowing my grandmother, it would be worse to show up in time and say the wrong thing than to be ten steps too late to say anything at all. My family members greeted me with tired smiles and big hugs. The children ignored or studied me. *This is what happens when you move away from home,* I thought. Your young family might never know who you are. I had been raised the way they were being raised now, and so I knew how it felt to have someone from out of town call themselves your family and to be stunned at the notion that family could be more than a twenty-minute drive away.

I sat in the lounge for a few minutes, catching up those who wanted to know what I'd been up to since moving away. I gave them the highlights.

Still working at the media company.

Still working on the book.

Kel and I had moved in together.

I did not give them the lowlights.

I'm broke.

I'm sad a lot.

I don't like my dream job anymore.

Grandma is going to die and I don't know what to do.

We all got quiet for a bit, mentally retreating back into our own most comfortable thoughts. I continued to sit with my family, looking around at all their faces, some I hadn't seen in years. For so long, I'd resented them. I felt they tethered me to that girl I didn't want to be anymore, and so I'd left. First to college, then to Indianapolis, and now New York. I felt more secure in myself than ever — certainly more than I'd felt under my mother's roof — but I still needed them. They were a part of me whether I acknowledged it or not.

My mother was adamant that all we had, and all we'd ever need, was family. If she was right, I had everything I needed. My mother, her four sisters, all of their children, and my grandmother lived in the same neighborhood. My cousins and I were raised like siblings who lived in different houses. My family had been around so much they became hard to escape. I dreamed of aunts and uncles who lived in other states, or even other countries, that I could visit in the summertime. Supposedly, everything I needed in the world was always a short walk from my room. Even then, I felt guilty about wanting more.

My cousins and I constantly joke about my grandmother's attempts to keep me close to home. "Ashley, why would you go away to school? Don't you know people get killed on college campuses every day?" "Did you know New York has ten rats for every person who lives there? You wanna live like that?" "You can always come home." My grandma was everything to me, but my fear of staying put would not be tempered.

There have been losses in the decision to leave home. When my sister's father died I could not hold her. When my cousins have babies, I am not there to visit them in the hospital. My grandmother was dying, and I was not there to sit with her and write down every hilarious and magical thing she said. I wasn't there to remember it all, every detail, for her. And for me too. But I was the only one who could figure out how to get my sister to her father's funeral. When I come home, my cousins get a break from their babies because I can't stop holding them. And when my grandmother needed someone to take over a bill or two, I was able to make that happen for her. Still, the feeling that I was failing them with the lack of physical presence never went away. If family was everything, the source of all that was needed to complete the picture, I was a willfully missing piece of the puzzle. And though I loved these people, I knew this was not my home anymore.

I sat in the waiting room feeling like a coward. What exactly was I afraid would happen to me when I saw her? That was the hard part. I didn't know. There was a convincing portion of my ability to reason that was resigned to the fact that indeed, my grandmother's death might kill me. Yes, I had known pain, but greater than this? I didn't think so. Every terrible thing that had ever happened to me, I would re-experience in real time if it gave my grandmother more time in this life.

I stood up, offered another round of hugs. A small mirror hung above the light switch in the doorway. I stopped there to reapply my lipstick. I pressed my lips together, and smiled to check for coverage. I used my fingers to separate the natural hair around my crown, knowing my grandmother won't like it, but wanting to feel like I looked nice. Just for me.

Her room was filled with more members of my family. My mother, brothers, sister, and a smattering of cousins formed a sloppy half circle around my grandmother's bed. The fluorescent lights gave each of them a thin gray mask, and before my eyes my family became a room of nervous mourning ghosts. They sat uncomfortably on the hyperfunctional and mostly taupe furniture. The adequately-padded chairs invited you to sit, but the cold steel bars protruding beneath the pads warned don't stay too long. Each person looked as if they'd rather be anywhere else. A room full of people bonded by blood and fear, and though I felt apart from them, for the first time in a long while, I did not feel alone.

The first person I saw, and hugged, was my mother. It was the right thing to do, and would have been noted if I hadn't done it. Then my sister walked over to me with open arms, and I opened mine to her as well. R.C. threw me a smile from the other side of the room and I tentatively smiled back, lamenting the wane in our closeness. I loved him then, as I always had, but we didn't know how to talk to each other anymore. I sensed a depth of pain in my brother I would not be allowed to explore, or attempt to remedy. I wasn't sure how much it had to do with me, but I knew the healing process wasn't mine to lead. If I'd learned anything being on my own these last few years, it was how much I needed this time away from my family to see myself clearly.

My grandmother lay in the bed, mouth agape, about fifty pounds lighter than she'd been at Christmas, and wigless. For as long as I'd been alive, she hadn't left the house without a hairpiece of some kind covering or clipped to her own short, curly hair. I stood immobile, startled by the fragile human that lay before me. She was my grandmother, and yet she was not. She was also a catfish, small and still, gills gasping, finding little to no respite, and trying anyway.

I moved over to her, trying to find a good spot among all the wires and humming medical devices. My lips connected with her cheek, and where they sunk into a firm softness only months ago, they now hit the steel of her cheekbone far too soon. She was alive, her labored breath a beating reminder, but the warmth was already slipping from the air hovering five inches above her shell. I did not shiver or recoil in the presence of her impending death, and I was proud of myself for not ruining the moment with my feelings. Her eyes fluttered, then opened wide. It took a moment to recognize me, but once she did, the corners of her mouth lifted slightly. She knew I was there.

"Hi, Grandma." I smiled at her with as much sincerity as I could muster. This was not a smiling time, and I did not want to lie with my face. But this wasn't about me. Her eyes slipped a little farther back, and then she was confused. She screwed up her face a bit, and assessed me from the corner of her eyes, before saying, "Quit being so weird." I turned to my sister and made a face. *There* she was. My sister's raised eyebrows and tilted head replied, *Same old Grandma.*

These were the moments we'd recount over family dinners and gatherings years after her passing. After we'd all filled our bellies with various food and drink, shared a few jokes, and maybe even danced to an old familiar song turned up loud, someone would say, "Remember when grandma used to . . . ?" and the rest of us would nod and laugh in recognition. We'd heard and shared these stories a million times before. There was always a story about Grandma. And everybody wanted to have the best story about some hilarious interaction with her. As I'd spent the most time with her, I usually had the best ones, and could confirm the details of everyone else's. For years, I'd kept a mental log of all our adventures, and I was determined to own the last of them as well.

In a way, it was comforting to have my grandmother be a little sharp with me from her deathbed. I always thought it was her sharpness that would keep her around. Who could die with that kind of fire coursing through their veins? But whatever burns will also burn up. Maybe it never made sense for anybody to run that hot for so long. Maybe, in her own way, she decided to drop that torch, and let the light fade. Maybe she was ready to go even if I wasn't ready for her to be gone.

My grandmother had been the matriarch of my family in every sense of the word. My siblings, cousins, aunts, and even family friends joked that she was the real version of Tyler Perry's Madea caricature. Not because she carried a gun, or spoke in an overemphasized accent, but because she kept us all together with hard language, good food, and stories of violence made into stomach-cramping laughs.

My mother, her four sisters, and even us kids could get into fights with one another whenever and however we wanted. We could yell and scream, punch and kick, and even drip bitter thoughts into phone lines crackling with rage, historic or newly discovered. We could curse one another and swear to never again be in one another's presence. Then my grandmother would have a family dinner. Where there was once tension, there would be full bellies and reluctant laughter. There would be music and somewhere for the children to go play on their own. If there was persistent arguing, my grandmother could and often did put a stop to it, reminding us that some things families just don't say to one another. Her love wasn't perfect, but she was nobody's caricature. There was no one on the planet like her.

My father wouldn't get to say goodbye to her, and the realization broke me down. He would never get to giggle with her about the boa constrictor she kept, and how much it scared him to find it roaming the house at night, broken free from its cage, and on the hunt. He would never get to apologize to her face for leaving her daughter alone with two children. He'd never get to explain to her that, no he hadn't been possessed by a demon. He'd committed a horrific crime and he'd paid for it with significant portions of all our lives, and that even that might not be payment enough. He couldn't be here for her, or me, or himself, and I wanted to scream.

As I turned away from my grandmother, a whole world in a dying body, my sister met me at the end of the hospital bed. We hugged again, and her own soft, natural hair brushed against my face, smelling like synthetic flowers and slow-warming sugar. Her arms, smaller than mine, held me tighter than I'd ever known her to hold anything or anyone. It was a moment, and it was a prayer.

"Are you all right?" I asked. I looked into her eyes, ready to find an answer there if she chose not to verbally provide one.

Just then, my grandmother opened her eyes and stared at us, both standing at the end of her bed. My sister and I turned to her. "Are you okay, Grandma? Do you need something?" Her eyes widened, and she stayed that way, silent and staring for several seconds. I stayed quiet.

If there was ever a time to make a memory, that time was now. And if I made this memory for myself, and this was the last time I saw her alive, and she saw me, what would I want her to see? I would want her to see me. All of me. Even the parts she would hate, just to give her the chance to see the full breadth of who I really was, and maybe, just for a moment, a real idea of who I might become. *You're going to miss it,* I thought. *I'm going to be so much better than I am now, and you're not going to be here to see it.*

My grandmother opened and closed her mouth, and the sound of her lips, dry from the work of breathing while dying, scraped like the meeting sides of a wrinkled brown paper bag. My mother leaned over and grabbed the cup filled with water, ice, and a white stick with a small square of green sponge stuck to the end. She soaked the sponge in and around the ice cubes, then lifted it to my grandmother's waiting mouth. Almost all of the water dissolved as the sponge met her papery lips, and the few drops that weren't immediately absorbed, rolled back onto her equally parched tongue. My mother did this, back and forth, swirling, lifting, and soothing her mother. Her face was soft, and ravaged.

When she finally could, my grandmother spoke to me and my sister, still waiting at her feet. "Your hair . . ." she started. My sister and I leaned in toward her at the same time. My grandmother's eyes began to water with frustration. "Your hair . . . is so beautiful." We looked at one another, shocked. She'd always disliked my hair, and my choice to go natural. She'd warned me that it would keep me from getting hired, keep me from finding a partner in life, and now, in the midst of her ultimate demise, she wanted me to know that actually, she loved my hair, as big and nappy and misshapen as it was.

I turned to my mother and asked her who was spending the night in the room that evening, after all other visitors would be asked to leave. She looked at me and said, "You should." I agreed.

After hugging everyone goodbye, I turned the taupe love seat into a bed for myself. I couldn't remember the last time my grandmother and I had slept in the same room, but I could remember many times before, from the beginning. I remembered falling asleep on her couch in the triplex, the warmth and scent of it as familiar as anything I'd ever known. I remembered sleeping in the same bed with her in Missouri, being read to from the bible each night, then falling asleep to the sounds of M*A*S*H. I remembered falling asleep in her lap during long bus rides, slumbering against her body at a New Year's Eve church revival, and sometimes just lying there, listening to her snore, wondering what could be wrong with a person's nose and throat to make that kind of sound. This night in the hospital, our last together, I hardly slept at all. Each time she moved, moaned, or my mind convinced me she needed me, I rose and reached for the cup, the sponge, and then, told my grandmother how much I loved her while trying to comfort her into a final rest.

My mother found me the next morning. I couldn't remember any other time in our lives where we cried so openly in front of one another. But on this day, for this woman we loved, we bawled without shame or restraint.

The shared act felt ancient, abundant, but it was unfamiliar. I stood in front of my mother, wanting to tell her that we didn't have time, that the time to be close was now, but all I could say was, "I'm not ready. Mama, I'm not ready." My mother surrounded me with her arms, and used the full force of them to shield me from the whole rest of the world.

"You are ready," she said. "You have to be, and you are."

Up until my grandmother died, I'd just accepted the way things were, resigned to my role as the member of my family no one quite understood. It had been enough, maybe even part of the fuel that kept me going in the warped way these things do sometimes, but now, I wanted more. I wanted their closeness. I wanted to start over, and let them see me as I am. I wanted to trust them. I wanted us to be as we are, people who love each other. I had a life and a home in New York with Kelly, but in so many ways, I'd abandoned my home here in Indiana. It didn't have to be this way. However complicated, I could exist in both, as me, fully me. I could be strong enough, because I had to be — if I didn't want to lose this. And I knew I didn't.

32

Kel and I were coming up on our first Christmas in our own space when my mother rang. Her voice sounded almost like my grandmother's as she said through the phone line, "You can always come home."

Our apartment was decorated for the holidays, and I wanted to start new traditions, make memories, and finally get started on a life that felt like it was mine. But when my mother told me my father was getting out of prison, I knew it was time to go home. I knew now that moving forward required going back. I flew to Indiana, and stayed for a week.

I wanted to be there as soon as my father got home, so I arrived at my aunt's house early. I'd begged my mother to come with me, and she had been so startled by the request that she'd obliged. When I asked, I hadn't thought about the fact that my mother hadn't seen my father in person for twenty-five years. Did she want to see him? I didn't know. But I knew I needed her with me. I'd spent a lot of time teaching myself not to need anyone, especially not my mother, but now I didn't care. I wanted her there.

She sat beside me, fidgeting nervously, but determined to be there the way I needed her to be. My heart burst with gratitude for her strength, and the love that kept her glued to her seat when I'm sure she would have rather been anywhere else.

As we waited, I realized this would be the first time I saw my parents in the same room. I'd heard them speak to one another on the phone a few times. I'd even read letters from him to her, ones clearly hidden or tucked away for safekeeping. My father always spoke of the great love he had for my mother, and my mother never spoke a word against him. Still, there was always pain bleeding into the space between them. He had betrayed her, betrayed us all, and his return didn't absolve him. We would all have so much to say to each other, so much to explain and release before we could have real or meaningful connections. Today was just the beginning.

My mother, aunt, uncle, and I sat around talking for over an hour before we heard the garage door open. I stood up — he didn't know I was there. He didn't even know I was coming to see him. There was no reason for me to stand, but I did.

I wanted to be the first person he saw, and I was.

He walked over to me silently, put his arms around me, and kissed my temple.

My aunt, composed and quiet seconds before, began to cry and yelled, "Thank you, Father God! Thank you, Jesus!" My uncle Clarence pulled out his phone and took dozens of photos. I could feel the buzz in my pocket as he sent them to me immediately. Within minutes, I had almost one hundred pictures of this one moment, this reunion, and introduction. More pictures of us together than I'd ever had before.

I looked at my father, and for a moment, I saw a reflection. I'd been the first to move away from my close-knit family, and it felt like I abandoned a part of myself. My life was split into befores and afters. How I am now and how my family would like to remember me has always been muddled by half-truths. And somewhere, in the center of it all, was my father's favorite girl.

It wasn't, and isn't, my place to forgive him for what's done. But my father is part of me, and I couldn't turn away from that. I couldn't turn away from him. I didn't want to.

We looked at each other, wondering who the other might be, excited to find out. It wasn't going to be easy — it never would have been. There was a new road to pave together, and I wanted to do the work beside him just as I am. Just as I've always been.

"Hi, Daddy," I said, and felt the first tear slither down the side of my face. He pulled me in closer. I pressed my cheek against his chest. I breathed in for four seconds, held it for seven, and let it out in eight.

This was my father, and I was his daughter. That was a good place to start.

Behind us my aunt cried, "God is so good!"

ACKNOWLEDGMENTS

It would be impossible to thank every single person who helped me find myself in this moment, but I'll consider this a good start.

Bryn Clark, my editor, has made a grievous mistake in striking the perfect balance between encouraging and challenging, and now she'll never get rid of me. Thank you for your patience, and your brilliant contributions. Thank you to my editorial, marketing, and publicity teams at Flatiron Books and An Oprah Book (Thanks, Oprah!). This was my publishing debut, and you all set a bar few even attempt to reach. And huge thanks to my amazing agent, Maria Massie, who knew I was worthy of a fantastic first book experience, and did everything in her power to make sure that's exactly what I got. Thank you to Hedgebrook for the writing residency that provided me with the literal space to finish my first draft of this book.

Thank you to my mother and father for loving me the best way you know how, and continuing to grow. Your faith in me gives me more faith in myself. To my siblings and niblings, still the best people I know in the whole world, thank you. I don't know how I got lucky enough to be this closely related to you, but I'm honored and grateful. I'm always on your side. Thank you to Billie, my grandmother, and all the stories she left me to tell for myself.

Thank you to my Muncie Family, Mitch, Becky, Charley, and Wilson. Thank you to the friends and loved ones who have walked beside me: Ashley Henderson, Spencer McNelly, Charla Yearwood, Danielle Daugherty, Daniel José Older, Eric Butler, Trent McFalls, Suleika Jaouad, Jill Christman, Cathy Day, Angel Nafis, Shira Erlichman, Rachel Syme, Diana Cenat, Zadie Smith, Stevi Waggoner, Tyson Mollison, and Brett Tubbs. And of course, Roxane Gay, my friend, mentor, and the shiniest star. Thank you, my friend, for clearing a path.

Aminatou Sow, Glennon Doyle, Saeed Jones, Isaac Fitzgerald, Laurie Halse Anderson, and John Green: thank you for sharing kind words about this book, my story, before it goes out into the world. You've made me so much less afraid, and so much more excited for sharing this work.

Last, but never least, thank you Kelly Glen Stacy for loving me so well, and making more than enough room for me to learn to love myself just as much. Thank you for re-arranging your life to support my dream, and holding me through it every step of the way. Everything's better when I'm with you, and you are here with me.

ABOUT THE AUTHOR

Ashley C. Ford has written or guest-edited for *Teen Vogue, New York* magazine, *The New York Times, Elle, BuzzFeed,* and many other web and print publications. She has been named among *Forbes* magazine's 30 Under 30 in Media and *Variety*'s New Power of New York. She lives in Indiana with her husband, Kelly Stacy, and their chocolate lab, Astro Renegade Ford-Stacy.